Suicide by Cop

James J. Drylie

Suicide by Cop

Scripted Behavior Resulting in Police Deadly Force

VDM Verlag Dr. Müller

Imprint

Bibliographic information by the German National Library: The German National Library lists this publication at the German National Bibliography; detailed bibliographic information is available on the Internet at http://dnb.d-nb.de.

Any brand names and product names mentioned in this book are subject to trademark, brand or patent protection and are trademarks or registered trademarks of their respective holders. The use of brand names, product names, common names, trade names, product descriptions etc. even without a particular marking in this works is in no way to be construed to mean that such names may be regarded as unrestricted in respect of trademark and brand protection legislation and could thus be used by anyone.

Cover image: www.purestockx.com

Publisher:
VDM Verlag Dr. Müller e. K., Dudweiler Landstr. 125 a, 66123 Saarbrücken, Germany,
Phone +49 681 9100-698, Fax +49 681 9100-988, Email: info@vdm-verlag.de

Copyright © 2007 VDM Verlag Dr. Müller e. K. and licensors
All rights reserved. Saarbrücken 2007

Produced in USA and UK by:
Lightning Source Inc., La Vergne, Tennessee, USA
Lightning Source UK Ltd., Milton Keynes, UK

ISBN: 978-3-8364-2842-2

Abstract

SUICIDE BY COP

by

James J. Drylie

This research will rely on an exploratory qualitative analysis of incidents (N=61) of police-

involved shootings resulting in the death or serious bodily injury of an aggressor who has

attacked the police with the apparent or stated intention of committing suicide. The use of a

collective case study analysis will be supported by descriptive analysis of the demographic

and situational characteristics of the suicidal actor in each of the cases that are determined

to be suitable for analysis. The central question in this research focuses on whether a

conceptualization of the phenomenon of suicide-by-cop can be developed from a

practitioner's perspective with a subordinate question that focused on whether the type or

kind of aggressive action used to provoke a police officer(s) into resorting to a deadly force

response was scripted? The research first developed a tripartite definition of SbC

delineating three distinct elements that must be present and can be clearly identified. A

conceptual model of how police practitioners view and understand SbC was developed

through a secondary analysis of individual case studies that were classified as SbC in the

preliminary studies. A secondary analysis, and subsequent classification of a case(s) as

SbC, required that the case file contain sufficient information regarding the actions of the

suicidal actor that supported the classification through the definitional litmus developed for

this research. In the final analysis of the data this research determined that a majority of the

original cases (N=57) that were originally classified as SbC did not meet the definitional criteria developed for this study, and a primary factor in many of these misclassifications was based on the erroneous assumption that the *actions* of the suicidal actor was the sole or principal determinant. Overall, less than half (45%) of the cases examined in the final analysis were classified as SbC, and in each of the 26 cases that met the definitional criteria of SbC evidence of scripted behavior by the suicidal actor was identified.

DEDICATION

This work is dedicated to the memory of two men whose values and principles served as an inspiration: To my father David Archibald Drylie for giving me the strength, physically, emotionally, and spiritually; and, to Professor James J. Fyfe for his professionalism and compassion.

ACKNOWLEDGEMENTS

I would like to first acknowledge my mentor Dr. Maria (Maki) Haberfeld for providing the necessary personal and academic direction that helped me to maintain the focus on my work in light of all of life's distractions. The opportunity to work under the tutelage of Dr. James Fyfe from the development of the proposal through the final draft of the dissertation was equally as rewarding. His insight into matters related to the use of deadly force as they related to suicide-by-cop helped my work to maintain a necessary objectiveness. In guiding the development of my research Dr. Dennis Kenney provided critical observations and direction. I would like to offer a special note of gratitude to Dr. Michael White who agreed to assist in the final defense of the dissertation after the untimely passing of Dr. Fyfe.

The work of several people in developing and maintaining the data on suicide-by-cop deserve particular recognition. The assistance of Dr. Robert Louden in opening several doors and finding the time to make the appropriate introductions within the academic community proved invaluable. The work of Dr. James Levine, former Executive Officer of the Doctoral Program, in cooperation with Dr. Anthony Pinnizotta and the FBI in securing the data set at John Jay College provided the foundation for this work to be considered. I would also like to note sincere appreciation to Dr. Dorothy Bracey for developing a level of academic discipline that enabled me to complete my studies; to Dr. Larry Sullivan for allowing me the opportunity to begin my research; and to Dr. Barry Spunt for his advice and counsel.

My experiences with friends and colleagues at John Jay were equally as rewarding. The sage advice offered early on by seasoned doctoral students Gerry LaSalle and Rick Fuentes has remained true to this day and I am grateful for their friendship. Particular thanks to three special people who helped make my experiences truly gratifying: John Laffey for being the voice of reason and helping in clearing the many hurdles; Kim Spanjol for being the kindest and most genuine person I ever met; and to Gennifer Furst for her insight.

Although an accomplishment such as this is often viewed as the work of one person I would like to express gratitude to each and every member of the West Orange Police Department, past and present, for the many words of encouragement and support that I have received these past few years in achieving this goal. The research for the writing of the dissertation did not occur in a vacuum and my experiences as a police officer in West Orange has helped me tremendously in completing this work.

Finally, special thanks go to my family. My wife Shannon has been unwavering in her support throughout my career and especially during my studies and each of my children, Kieran, Nolan, Sean, and Jamie has encouraged me to pursue my dream. All of this would not have been possible if it were not for two very important and extraordinary women: My mother Pat for being there from the beginning, and to my mother-in-law Sharon who has opened her heart to me in a very special way.

TABLE OF CONTENTS

LIST OF TABLES

Chapter 1

*The progress of a science is proven by the progress toward
solution of the problem it treats.* Emile Durkheim (1897).

INTRODUCTION

The purpose of this research is to examine the phenomenon of suicide-by-cop (SbC) with

the expectation of developing a clearer understanding of how the phenomenon is viewed in

a generalized sense by police practitioners. This generalized view will be developed into a

conceptualization of the phenomenon that will be tested using specific SbC definitional

criteria to determine how closely, if at all, the generalized view held by practitioners of

SbC compares to these criteria. A necessary element of this research will be the

establishment of a clear distinction between SbC and other police involved shootings (Fyfe,

2004), a point that will be discussed at length throughout this paper.

This research is a collective case study analysis (Stake, 2003) of incidents of police-

involved shootings resulting in the deaths or serious bodily injury of aggressors who attack

the police with the stated or apparent intention of committing suicide. The study will be

supported by descriptive analysis of the demographic and situational characteristics

associated with the suicidal actor in each of the cases that are determined to be suitable for

analysis. It is not the intention of this research to evaluate the practices and procedures of

the police personnel involved in the incident or in any subsequent investigation. It is

anticipated that what is learned from this research will serve as a source of information for

future examinations of the use of deadly force by police officers, specifically in scenarios

that potentially may result in SbC.

The research will be conducted using a two-pronged approach that will begin with the construction of a specific definition of SbC for the purpose of this study. Using the extant literature as a foundation, a tripartite definition of SbC will be developed for this research so that the cases examined in this study can be viewed through an objective lens. The elements of this definition will narrowly focus on the intent and subsequent actions of the suicidal actor. Intent of the suicidal actor will not be viewed as axiomatic merely because the actor pointed a weapon at or in the direction of a police officer(s) or a third-party. The research design will require that evidence of suicidal intent involving a police use of deadly force vis-à-vis verbal or non-verbal communication can be determined from the file, the possession and threat, attempt, or use of some form of lethal weapon by the suicidal actor, and a provocation of the police can be objectively determined.

The second prong of this research will consist of developing a conceptual model of how SbC is perceived in a generalized sense by practitioners moving to a more specific measurement (Maxfield and Babbie, 1995) that is intended to test the strength of that model against the constructed definition. This prong will rely on a secondary analysis of individual case studies of police-involved shootings that occurred in various jurisdictions across the United States in an effort to gain better understanding of how the phenomenon is viewed by these practitioners. These initial case studies were conducted by police officers in an academic setting and the analysis was independent of any criminal or civil legal proceedings. The analysis of these cases by the submitting officers resulted in a classification of the case by the submitting officer as SbC, or in a limited number of cases, attempted SbC. This research will seek to examine these case studies in an effort to determine if the phenomenon SbC, as perceived by this group of practitioners, can be supported by scientific analysis.

This study will examine data collected through the efforts of the Federal Bureau of Investigation (FBI) on 61 cases involving the use of deadly force by police in instances wherein the actions of the decedent were believed to have been an initiator provoking a deadly force response by police. The files, which were accumulated over a period of years by staff of the Behavioral Science Unit (BSU) at the FBI Academy, Quantico, VA, are non-random in nature and were collected from police agencies across the United States. The SbC case files are a smaller subset of a larger collection of police files on crimes of violence, specifically homicide, sexual assault, serial crimes, and pedophilia, that were similarly collected by the FBI for a larger unrelated project.

The data originated with police officers attending various classes and seminars held at the FBI National Academy (NA)[1] that focused both historically and contemporaneously on violence in American society. The officers submitted the files with minimal requirements or specificity as to what constituted SbC, and no definition of suicide-by-cop was offered as a guide. The absence of standardized guidelines in this regard was problematic when reviewing the data and will be discussed in detail in the conclusion of this paper.

The officers attending these classes and seminars were doing so as a part of a national training program offered through the FBI. The NA originated in 1935 under the direction of the FBI as a training program for local, county and state law enforcement officers, and was

---

[1] The courses and seminars that were a vehicle for collecting the data contained in the files are spread over a period of approximately ten years. A more exact range will be determined upon a final review of the files and reported in the analysis.

designed as a national training center. Presently, the University of Virginia awards a certificate to attendees at the NA who successfully complete 13 semester hours of course work with a passing grade.

The mission of the NA as noted in the *General Instructions* issued to the attendees of the 205th Session (April 1, 2001 – June 8, 2001) is:

> "To support, promote, and enhance the personal and professional development of experienced law enforcement officers by providing relevant education and training and to increase their information networks in order to prepare them for increasingly complex and dynamic leadership roles in the law enforcement community" (F.B.I., November 27, 2000).

As noted in the mission statement, the NA focuses on experienced law enforcement officers, and it will be this level of law enforcement experience that will form the foundation for a conceptualization of SbC.

SbC Data

The data consist of copies of police files documenting police involved shootings wherein the actions of the decedent were later categorized as intentionally provoking with the expectation of a deadly force response by the police for the purpose of causing the death of the aggressor. A preliminary review of the files helped to determine the span of time covered by these cases, the representativeness of types of law enforcement agencies and geographic regions, a categorization of the types of incidents involving a police response or presence, and frequencies of the types of weapons involved.

The dates of the cases in the files range from 1979 through 2003 and involve law enforcement jurisdictions that can be classified as urban, suburban, and rural, ranging in size from small agencies to large. Various law enforcement agencies including municipal,

4

county, state, and federal are represented with cases occurring in 27 states in all four

regions of the United States. The dispersion of cases occurring in these states range from

the lower of one case per state (n=15) to the highest of six cases per state (n=1).

Preliminarily, it has been determined that the most frequent reason for an initial police

response in any of these cases was due to a 9-1-1 call of a suicidal person (n=9). Domestic

violence (n=8) was the next most prevalent initiator of a police response closely followed

by reports of a person armed with a gun (n=7). The incidence of cases involving the

commission of a felony (n=6) included crimes such as homicide, armed robbery, and bank

robbery. The remaining cases will be similarly categorized. However, this will require a

thorough analysis that will be discussed in Chapter 4. The use of a firearm, including

unloaded and replica weapons, was found in the vast majority of cases (n=43). Knives

(n=9) were used with significantly less frequency, and in four cases the use of some other

type of weapon other than a gun or knife was identified. Overall, the case files were found

to contain extensive copies of police and medical reports, including psychological

evaluations, medical histories, and autopsy reports, statements of family, friends, and

witnesses, crime scene photographs and diagrams, transcripts of telephone conversations

and police-audio tapes, as well as news articles from local newspapers covering the initial

story.

One of the prerequisites for inclusion in the original data set, as established by the FBI, is

that the case is closed. In each of the files there exists a cover sheet containing limited

situational and demographic variables that are related to the incident. The majority of files

contain a synopsis of the incident as described by the submitting officer. Evidence of a

detailed case analysis by the submitting officer is found only in a limited number of the more recent files. The absence of any type of abstract, synopsis, or analysis in a file(s) will not preclude the use of that file for inclusion in developing the proposed conceptual model. Omissions of this type require the secondary analysis to focus solely on the case without the benefit of any insight or thought on the part of the submitting officer. This did not prevent cases from being excluded from analysis. However, the determination of what factors led the initial case study to be classified SbC by the submitting officer had to be extracted from the file.

Cases studies that show an analysis of the incident beyond a mere reporting of the situational and demographic variables will help to determine the level of strength in the classification of SbC, and will be a primary source of information in developing a conceptualization of SbC.

The scope of the research will be limited to examining specific cases of SbC found in the data that meet specific definitional criteria developed for this study. The specificity of the definitional criteria will be discussed more completely in Chapter 4.

Of the 61 cases examined a few selected to illustrate specific points will be presented in a detailed narrative to allow for an understanding of the dynamics of a suicide wherein the intended or expected mechanism for death is a deadly force response by the police.

Presently, the data set is stored within the campus of John Jay College of Criminal Justice. The Institutional Review Board (IRB) of John Jay and the IRB of the FBI have approved this data set for use in analysis. Due to confidentiality restrictions set by the FBI, information from the data set cannot be reproduced wherein the identities of any of the persons involved would be revealed. These restrictions include a prohibition in identifying

the instructors of any particular course or seminar, and/or the specific course or seminar

where the data was collected. Additionally, follow-up contacts with any of the parties

involved or identified in the files are prohibited. These restrictions create a necessary

delimitation on the scope of this research (Creswell, 2003).

Notwithstanding the significance of the involvement of other players in the SbC drama,

specifically law enforcement agents, the focus of this research will limit itself to an in-

depth examination of the actions and reactions of the suicidal actor in the presence of a

police response to the use of deadly force.

Provoking a Deadly Force Response by Police
The underlying theory for this research is based in the belief that a suicidal person who opts

to provoke or initiate a police use of deadly force response as a mechanism of death is

doing so according to generalized societal expectations. These expectations of a police

response to life-threatening behavior are anticipated to ensure a successful end result --

death. A person who has suicidal ideations that involve a mechanism of death using a

police response to deadly force may well have formulated a plan of actions and reactions to

an anticipated police response that is expected to cause the suicidal actors death. This

anticipated response, according to Dwyer, Graesser, Hopkinson, and Lupfer, allows the

person in this drama to "make inferences about how the event will 'turn out' and adapt his

or her behavior accordingly" (1990. p. 296). The inference of how future actions will

proceed become a *script*, "a cognitive structure or framework that, when activated,

organizes a person's comprehension of stereotypic situations, allowing the person to have expectations and to make inferences about the potential outcome of a set of events"

(Dwyer, et al., 1990. p. 296).

Cognitive psychologists define this structure, or script, "as the mental representation of an activity that a person enacts frequently or in a cognitive manner" (Dwyer, et al., 1990. p. 296). The psychological script theory will be the foundation upon which this research will be built. Individualized cases will be reviewed in an attempt to determine if sufficient information exists that demonstrates evidence of suicidal ideation or planning involving a provoked police response of deadly force. Demonstrative evidence in this regard can then be used to develop the foundation for associating SbC with scripted behavior.

Defining Suicide

Suicide is one of four *modes* of death that also include mortality by natural, accidental, or homicidal means (Geberth, 1993, p. 572). The *manner of death* would be the mechanism or instrumentality (e.g., gunshot; blunt trauma) that was used to cause the death. The *cause* of death is the "pathological condition which produced the death." (p. 571) The interests of the present research are both the mode of death, in this case suicide, and the manner of death, which is the police use of deadly force in response to the initiated actions and or provocations of a suicidal actor that resulted in the death or serious bodily injury of the actor.

Durkheim (1951) applies the term suicide to, "any death which is the direct or indirect result of a positive or negative act accomplished by the victim himself" (p. 42). This definition, in Durkheim's view is not complete, and like some many other definitions, does not differentiate between suicide of the insane, the delusional, or individuals experiencing

8

hallucinations from the person who is cognizant of their actions (p. 43). An equally vexing question in this regard would be, "Shall suicide be considered to exist only if the act resulting in death was performed by the victim to achieve this result" (p. 43)? An affirmative answer to Durkheim's question simply negates the SbC phenomenon, but the answer to this question still remains to be seen.

Abbott, Young, Grant, Goward, Seager, Pugh, and Ludlow (2003) suggest, "That there is no universally agreed definition of suicide or attempted suicide " (p.1). The author's view suicide as involving an "intentional action resulting in the taking of one's life" (p.1). The problem, according to O'Connor and Sheehy (2000), is determining the intent of the suicidal person. Similarly, Simon, Swann, Powell, Potter, Kresnow, and O'Carroll (2001) note similar definitional problems with studies focusing on characteristics of impulsivity associated with suicide attempts and attempters. The estimates of the proportion of impulsive suicide attempts will vary widely based on the definitions used as well as the samples that are studied (2001: p. 49).

Allen (2001) relies on a definition of suicide, which focuses on causation, that is offered by the *Suicide Prevention Training Program* of the Miami-Dade Police Department that incorporates principles found in learning theory. This definition identifies suicide as a mechanism for problem solving with the following aims: 1) to improve an unpleasant and untenable situation, 2) improve a threatened self-image and 3) exercising omnipotence instead of hopelessness and helplessness (2001).

General Data on Suicide

The act of suicide is final and the effect of the suicidal actor's actions upon others can be profound, widespread, and long lasting (Goldney, 2004). The suicide of a person at the hands of the police can have a devastating effect on a multitude of people. The surviving family and friends of the suicidal person are affected along with the community (Crosby, Cheltenham, and Sachs, 1999), and the police officer and their families, colleagues, and department.

Gliatto and Rai (2004) have described the spectrum of suicidal behavior as ranging from suicidal thoughts to a completed act. Yearly in the United States the number of suicides is approximately 30,000, and 3,000 deaths in Canada are classified as suicides annually (Heinsen, 2001). These numbers are disturbing considering that in 1950 the number of suicides in the United States was reported to be approximately 17,000 (Henry and Short, 1954). Today, worldwide the number reaches one million (Goldsmith, 2002).

Adjusting for age, the national suicide rate is approximately 11.1 per 100,000 "making it the ninth leading cause of death in the United States" (Crosby et al., 1999, p. 131). [2] According to Kachur, Potter, James, and Powell the "age-adjusted suicide rate has remained remarkably constant since the 1940s (1995. p.1). A recent study by the New Jersey Department of Health revealed that suicide among 15-24 year olds is the third-leading cause of preventable death in the state (Stewart, 2004), and accounts for 11 % of the deaths for this age group nationally (Morrison and L'Heureux, 2000). The Office of Juvenile Justice and Delinquency Prevention and the Centers for Disease Control and

---

[2] These data were based on statistics provided by the National Center for Health Statistics in 1995 (Crosby et al., 1999). Recently released data on the national rate have revealed a drop to 10.5 per 100,000 (Stewart, 2004).

Prevention (CDC) report that four per cent of the suicides in the United States between 1981 and 1998 were committed by persons under the age of 18 (2004).

Some of the common motives for suicide according to Shamoo and Patros (1990) are:

- The person is seeking help;
- They wish to escape an intolerable situation;
- Looking to get relief from a terrible state of mind;
- An attempt to influence another person;
- Trying to make others feel sorry for them; and/or
- Desire to die.

These motives are not mutually exclusive of each other, and can in some cases co-exist (Fyfe, 2004).

The number of attempted suicides far surpasses these figures. According to Goldsmith (2002) the number of persons treated in hospital emergency rooms annually as a result of an attempted suicide is 21 times greater than the approximately 30,000 annual suicides numbering approximately 650,000 annually (p. 17). Hardy and Cull (1973) note, "Persons who make dramatic gestures may succeed in killing themselves even though this may have been neither their desire nor their intention" (p. 224).

Obviously the suicide rate is an issue that has, and continues to receive, a great deal of analysis and is an issue that has far reaching implications for any society.

Police Use of Force

The second factor related to this research is the use of force, specifically deadly force by the police. Throughout the history of policing the use of force, particularly deadly force, by and against the police, has been a subject of interest and concern to many different and diverse groups within our society. The police and violence, according to Sherman (1980) "are central to our conception of government" (p. 1). The police are guardians of society, and as such are authorized to use force to meet and overcome that level of force that they encounter.

The extraordinary powers vested in the police in accomplishing the police mission have been noted from one century to the next (Kinnaird, 2003; Vollmer, 1972). These powers, dating back to the early formation of police agencies in the United States, did not originally include the option to use deadly force, although the "unique authority to use force in situations where it is necessary for self-defense, to lawfully arrest a suspect, or to prevent criminal activity" (Blumberg and Kreisel, 2003, p. 148) has been a mainstay of American policing since the beginning.

The City of New York officially adopted an ordinance creating a police department on May 23, 1845. It was not until some twelve years later in November 1857 that the police officers working in New York City, after a state takeover of the department, began to carry firearms (Lardner and Reppetto, 2000).

Sherman attributes the growth of the paradox of policing violence to two points in the Nation's history. The first point was as a result of the mass production of the revolver after the Mexican-American War and the proliferation of these weapons into mainstream

America after that war. The second point, according to Sherman, occurred as the Reform

Era of policing gave way to the Professional Era in the early part of the Twentieth Century.

Sherman credits the birth of police tactics intended to cope with exotic weapons used by

organized crime elements during that time as a form of "glorification" (p. 3) that "may have

given a high level of social approval to the violence the police used" (p.3).

Rumbaut and Bittner (1979) in citing Bittner (1970) describe the police role as "a

mechanism for the distribution of situational justified force in society" (p. 265). Bittner

elaborates in the following passage from a previous work:

> "There can be no doubt that this feature of police work is uppermost in the minds of
> the people who solicit police aid or direct attention of the police to problems, that
> the persons against whom the police proceed have this feature in mind and conduct
> themselves accordingly, and that every conceivable police intervention projects the
> message that force may be, and may have to be, used to achieve a desired
> objective" (1970, pp. 40-41).

Friedrich (1980) views the use of force by police as theoretically important as it affects the

attitudes and behaviors of the public not only toward the police, but also toward

government in a general sense. Friedrich approaches the subject by classifying the use of

force by police into three distinctly differing approaches. The *individual approach* views

use of force in terms of the individual officer. The personal and psychological makeup of

the officer would be factors that need to be considered in analyzing the application of force

by an officer. Another type of approach, according to Friedrich is *situational*. This

approach accounts for the type, level, and degree of force used by an officer(s) based on

situational characteristics. A third type of approach is *organizational*. Here the level, type,

and degree of force can be viewed as a by-product of the organization. Any one, a

combination, or all three of these factors may present during a deadly force confrontation,

13

and the ability to isolate or definitively identify a specific approach would be very problematic.

Use of force situations tends to be dynamic, fluid incidents with decisions made by involved officers that are highly subjective, and "the use of deadly force by the police is generally very controversial" (Hontz, 2000, p. 462). The frequency of shootings involving the police is rare (Alpert and Dunham, 1995; Geller and Scott 1992; Yarmey 1990) when compared to the number of encounters between the police and public that occurs each year (Horvath, 1987). However, the consequences of a police-involved shooting can be devastating in terms of the impact on the community (Geller and Scott, 1992), and these consequences are often times irreversible (Yarmey, 1990). Geller and Scott (1992) summarize the issue best in their work on police-involved shootings:

> "The importance of police-involved shootings stems not so much from their frequency (they are rare compared with the hundreds of thousands of encounters each year between police and persons suspected of violating the law) but from their potential consequences. Any experienced police officer knows the potentially devastating effects of even justified shootings by police—loss of life and bereavement, risks to an officer's career, the government's liability to civil suits, strained police-community relations, rioting, and all the economic and social crises that attend major civil disturbances" (p.1).

The mission of policing in the United States is altruistic. The variations of the motto *to protect and serve* can be found in police policy manuals, on the sides of marked police vehicles, and in insignia and memorabilia across the Nation. However, notwithstanding the altruism associated with the police mission, officers are vested with the power and authority to use coercive force (Adams, 1999; U.S. Department of Justice, 1996), including deadly force, in accomplishing this mission. The force used against the police is considered to be the influencing factor in the decision to use force, and to what level (Garner,

14

Buchanan, Schade, and Hepburn, 1996). Toward this end, the use of force by police is a considerable demonstration of the powers afforded to police within our society (Kinnaird, 2003).

That the police are authorized to use lethal force is axiomatic, and the authority to do so is based in common law (Dwyer, et al., 1990). The use of force by the police is expected to be reasonable and is grounded within democratic principles. Whether a person is cognizant of a police response in a deadly force encounter from personal experience, socialization, or through media exposure[3] (Alpert and Dunham, 1995), the knowledge base is generally the same; people are well aware that police officers can and will defend themselves or third parties when deadly force is threatened or used. A further consideration in this regard is the means the officers will resort to when threatened by a firearm or other type of lethal weapon is most often the police service revolver or pistol. According to Miller (2002), the police are an obvious mechanism for suicidal persons due to the fact that they, the police, are armed, trained, and authorized to use deadly force if threatened.

The emergence of SbC as a phenomenon
In the early- to mid-1980s a phenomenon began to emerge in the United States that involved the use of force, more specifically lethal force, by police officers or similar law enforcement agents. It was gradually becoming evident that people within society were successfully using a law enforcement response as a means to an end. The desired end for these individuals was death at the hands of the police. The means to this end was an

---

[3] Alpert and Dunham note that the portrayal of the police use of firearms in popular media is based less on reality than on the financial concerns of entertainment industry.

anticipated police response. This response was the use of deadly force by the police to a real or perceived threat posed by the suicidal actor.

For a variety of reasons people are committing what is ostensibly considered to be suicide at the hands of police. These individuals are manipulating police officer(s) into using lethal force by threatening violent behavior that is prompting a deadly force response by these very same police officer(s). In some instances the threat is real such as in pointing a loaded handgun or other type of firearm in the direction of an officer(s) on scene, or by firing the weapon directly at or in the presence of the officer(s). In other cases the threat, as real as the officer(s) and others may perceive it, is in fact a fabrication, a ruse, intended to provoke a lethal response from the police. In either of these generalized scenarios the motive of the actor is at times obvious, although not always; the use of deadly force by the officer(s) in response to a real or perceived threat is intended to cause the suicidal actor's death, specifically at the hands of the police. However, not all police involved shootings fall within this category, and it will not always be axiomatic that the use of deadly force against the police is a suicidal act. Geller and Scott (1992) note that this difficulty in classification arises when researchers attempt to compare data across jurisdictional boundaries. The lack of standardization in reporting and recording pertinent information by the various police agencies leads to ambiguity and inaccuracy. Herein lies one of the many problems with clearly defining and identifying incidents in this manner.

In their examination of the problems associated with the lack of clarity of a definition for SbC Pinnizotta, Davis and Miller (2005) note the increasing frequency in which the term is used by police, the general public, and the media. Consider the following points offered by

Pinnizotta et al. that underscore the current ambiguity of the phenomenon:

> "If an offender points an unloaded firearm at a police officer who, in turn, kills that
> person, what facts and circumstances must be present and reported to enable
> agencies to determine that the incident was a suicide by cop? Did the offender
> deliberately point a firearm at an officer knowing it was not loaded? Or, was it
> merely an oversight and the offender meant to kill the officer? Obviously, and
> incident of this nature needs a thorough investigation to arrive at an accurate
> determination" (2005, p. 10).

Another problem with the ambiguity of the term SbC aside from vagueness is something

more troubling. Can SbC be prompted or exacerbated by a particular police response?

More specifically, Fyfe (2004) questions if SbC is "just an after-the-fact way of explaining

sloppy police work?" Fyfe's question raises legitimate legal and academic concerns. The

possibility exists that poor or inadequately planned police tactics can exacerbate an already

tenuous situation (Fyfe and Blumberg, 1985). Prior to cited discussions on SbC found in

the literature Fyfe and Blumberg question the role of police tactics in situations dealing

with certain situations prompting what Fyfe (1986) considers unnecessary police violence.

This point is raised by Fyfe and Blumberg in the following passage:

> "Some killings by police, for example, occur when officers act in tactically
> inappropriate ways, and subsequently find themselves in imminently life-
> threatening situations that require them to shoot to survive. Some officers have
> forced open doors behind which they knew lurked lone knife wielding mentally
> disturbed persons, and have had to take lives in order to save their own. In such
> cases, we should ask whether attempting instead to wait out such persons would not
> have been more advisable" (1985, p. 114).

As sound as Fyfe and Blumberg's (1985) points are the research design developed for this

study will exclude cases where the actions of the police are determined to be offensive and

thereby provoking the actor into action.

CHAPTER 2

The studies conducted on suicide-by-cop (SbC) to date have been limited in number

beginning in the mid- to late-1990s. These studies are preceded temporally by a small

number of references to SbC by practitioners in the police, medical, and legal professions,

and an even smaller number of academics. There seems to be a general consensus that the

identification of the phenomenon emerged in the early- to mid-1980s, but to date, no source

within the literature that clearly delineates how, where, or when this phenomenon began

was found. It could logically be argued that suicidal actors resorted to the provocation of

the police for the purpose of causing death of the actor long before this. However, the

practices of the police, legal and general social cultures before this period in examining the

connection of police use of force incidents and the motivation of the actor may not have

been as probative, or the phenomenon may well have simply been overlooked.

The literature review for this study was designed to examine SbC in the totality of the

incident, including the views scholars and practitioners have on the complexities of suicide

and possible measures to reduce it. The material examined in Section I of this chapter will

outline a general discussion on the theories associated with the understandings of suicide,

beginning with the work of Émile Durkheim. Section II will be an in-depth examination of

the literature on SbC.

Previous studies on SbC have concentrated primarily on the dynamics of the violence

between the suicidal person and the responding officer in a macro-level analysis. However,

this study will rely on a micro-level analysis of the actions, and more particularly the verbal and/or non-verbal communications of the suicidal actor prior to and during a SbC incident, and will attempt to determine if these communications evidence a level of planning or scripted behavior on the part of the suicidal actor. The presence of communication of the intent to commit SbC, pre- or post-incident, coupled with the criteria associated with script theory, will be used to construct a specific definition that will be used as a gauge to clearly identify the cases found within the data examined for this research.

I)   Suicide

The term suicide-by-cop (SbC) is intended to describe an action wherein a person, a suicidal actor, manipulates a police officer(s) into using deadly force to cause the death of the suicidal actor. The following definition of SbC is perhaps the most commonly accepted:

> "(A) police colloquialism used to describe incidents in which individuals, bent on self-destruction, engage in life-threatening and criminal behavior in order to force the police to kill them" (Geberth, 1996, p. 389).

The term suicide-by-cop itself can be confusing, and may lead some into mistakenly visualizing a scenario in which a police officer takes his or her own life. In order to properly discuss SbC there is the need to place the term within boundaries that will isolate it from "similar phenomena" and any possibility of confusion is removed (Hart, 2003, p. 129). Similarly, Durkheim (1951) raises this caution. According to Durkheim, "everyday language," (p. 41) when not properly defined, is susceptible to multiple meanings, and "too imprecise for serious scientific argument." (Hart, 2003, p. 129) Toward this end it becomes necessary to first discuss suicide in a general sense in order to learn from the scholars and theorists who have studied this subject with a great deal of specificity. It is here that we

19

must look to see if there is any nexus in the earlier studies of suicide, including the classification of behavior that is obviously self-destructive (Ellis, 1988), and the current phenomenon of SbC.

The literature is replete with references to the work on suicide conducted by Durkheim from 1890 through 1897 when his work, *Suicide,* was first published (Hawthorn, 1976). In his works *The Division of Labor* and *Suicide,* Durkheim is credited with laying the foundation of the sociologically based theory of anomie (Wallace, 2000), and it is his work on suicide that is considered "an historical anchorpoint" (sic) (Futrell, 1974, p. 3) for subsequent studies on this phenomenon (p. 3). Kreitman (1988) categorizes Durkheim's work on suicide as being "immensely fertile" (p. 69), notwithstanding criticism, and that the work, with any shortcomings, is still widely referred to. Unnithan, Huff-Corzine, Corzine, and Whitt (1994) credit Durkheim's work in *Suicide* has having more influence on sociologists as well as social scientists than "any other single volume" (p. 4).

Durkheim's theory on anomie begins with an absence of social control, such as is the case when there are fluctuations, positive or negative, in the economy. The absence of social controls due to these fluctuations then leads to anomie resulting in an inability to fulfill one's goals. Frustration then develops, which often results in deviance. The ultimate form of deviance according to Durkheim's theory is suicide (Wallace, 2000).

The presence of anomie contributes toward the potential for suicidal action, and it is here that Durkheim identifies three categories of suicide. According to Durkheim (1951) suicide would fit one of the following categories:

"Egoistic suicide results from mans no longer finding a basis for existence in life; altruistic suicide, because this existence appears to man situated beyond life itself. The third sort of suicide, the existence of which has been shown, results from man's activities lacking regulation and his consequent suffering. By virtue of its origin we shall assign this last variety the name of *anomic suicide* (emphasis in original work). (p. 258)

Durkheim does identify a fourth category of suicide, fatalistic suicide (Futrell, 1994).

However, Durkheim openly dismisses this category. Durkheim describes fatalistic suicide

as:

" . . . a type of suicide the opposite of anomic suicide, just as egoistic and altruistic suicides are opposites. It is the suicide deriving from excessive regulation, that the person with futures pitilessly blocked and passions violently choked by oppressive discipline. It is the suicide of very young husbands, of the married woman who is childless. So, for completeness sake, we should set up a fourth suicidal type. But it has little contemporary importance and examples are so hard to find aside from the cases just mentioned that it seems useless to dwell upon it. However it might be said to have historical interest. Do not the suicides of slaves, said to be frequent under certain conditions, belong to this type, or all suicides attributed to excessive physical or moral despotism? To bring out the ineluctable and inflexible nature of a rule against which there is no appeal, and in contrast with the expression "anomy" (sic) which has just been used, we might call it *fatalistic suicide* (emphasis added in original text). (p.276)

Although Durkheim discounted fatalistic suicide as not having contemporary importance at

the time, in the 1890s (p. 276), it may well figure more prominently in the present-day

analysis of incidents of SbC. Durkheim describes fatalistic suicide as being derived from

excessive regulation, futures that are blocked for some reason or another, and the chucking

of passions by oppressive discipline. These very reasons for suicide may well be found in

the various typologies and classifications of SbC as noted in this literature review.

Durkheim's work on suicide, which was based on official statistics (Kreitman, 1988;

McIntosh, 1991), has produced a tradition in research on the subject (Liska and Messner,

1999), and has been categorized as a work that presents "the most satisfactory and understandable explanation" on the problem of suicide (Lunden, 1973, p. 395-6)[4].

However, Durkheim's work with suicide has received limited mention in the SbC

literature, and references, in this sense, are for the most part definitional (Grella, 2000;

Parent, 1992; Parent, 2004).

In defining suicide, Durkheim was careful not to attribute reason or motive to the act

(Hawthorn, 1976). In discussing the suicidal act Durkheim states: "The intrinsic nature of

the acts so resulting is unimportant" (1951:42). However, Simpson in the *Editor's*

Introduction to *Suicide* discusses the "interconnectedness of suicide with social and natural

phenomena" (1951), and it is this theory of interconnectedness that may hold the key for

understanding the reasoning and motive behind suicidal acts that culminate in an SbC

incident.

Suicide, as defined by Durkheim (1951) is a death that results directly or indirectly from

the affirmative actions of the suicidal person (actor)[5], who would have the expectation of

that action resulting in their death. Suicide, according to Durkheim, is the result of either a

positive or negative act on the part of the actor. A positive act would involve some form of

"muscular energy" (p. 42) resulting in an act of violence. In contrast, a negative act could

be a "refusal to take food," which is viewed "as suicidal as self-destruction by a dagger or

fire-arm [sic]" (p. 42). However, Durkheim does not complete the definition of suicide as

an act committed solely by the actor. It is here that he raises issues that are extremely

pertinent to the discussion of SbC:

---

[4] Lunden can be found in Mannheim, H. (1973). Pioneers in Criminology. Montclair, NJ. Patterson Smith.

[5] In the defining suicide Durkheim identifies the suicidal person as a "victim." The term "actor" will be used
  in this paper to avoid any confusion.

"Shall suicide be considered to exist only if the act resulting in death was performed by the victim to achieve this result? Shall only he be thought truly to slay himself who has visited who has wished to do so, and suicide be intentional self-homicide? In the first place, this would define suicide by a characteristic which, whatever its interest and significance, would at least suffer from not being easily recognizable, since it is not easily observed. How discover the agent's motive and whether he desired death itself when he formed his resolve, or had some other purpose? Intent is too intimate a thing to be more than approximately interpreted by another." (1951, p. 43)

Durkheim raises several questions in this passage that are relevant to previous as well as current examinations of SbC. Wilson, Davis, Bloom, Batten, and Kamara (1998) examined discrepancies of pathologists in determining the manner of death of 15 cases. This study, which will be discussed in detail in this chapter, found that cases that were described, as SbC were, the majority of the time, classified as homicide. It may well be argued that Durkheim's point in this passage is to identify the gaps in defining suicide as the result of an act performed solely by the actor. He identifies cases wherein a soldier in combat commits an act that most likely will result in certain death for the purpose of saving others. Nor does he view the mother who sacrifices herself for her children's safety committing an unnatural act (p. 43). These acts are of desperation, but desperation of a differing sort than that of the suicidal actor. The intent of the soldier or the mother is preservation of others at the extreme price of self-sacrifice. Durkheim argues that the intent of a suicidal actor is personal and should be loosely interpreted, but this position does not consider when suicide becomes a public act such as in the case of SbC. Defining the phenomenon will require more than an approximation that may or may not interpret intent of the actor.

Durkheim sees the act of suicide as one of desperation, with the furtherance of life not being an option. In this sense suicide is perceived as a solution to a problem for the individual, whose feeling of helplessness would be solved when the pain they are feeling, for however long, is ended (Brewster, 2001).

Durkheim's theory on suicide stemmed from his belief in a state of "normlessness" or "deregulation" (McCaghy, Capron, and Jamieson, 2000, p. 57) that existed within society, and that suicide was predicated on societal properties as opposed to those of the individual (McCaghy, Capron, and Jamieson, 2000). According to Hart (2003), Durkheim was not overly concerned with the individual action of a person resulting in suicide, anomie, for Durkheim, "referred to a condition of relative normlessness in a society or group" (Merton, 1968, p. 215). In this sense, Durkheim was interested in proving that suicide was a social phenomenon. This position by Durkheim may account for the lack of an examination of the suicidal act and the meaning of the selection of the manner of death by the suicidal actor.

The key to the explanation of suicide for Durkheim was economic change within the larger environs of society (Liska and Messner, 1999). Anleu (1995) describes Durkheim's study as an "enterprise to delineate an exclusively sociological subject matter amenable to scientific analysis" (p. 13). From this it can be shown that although suicide tends to be an individualistic act, the acts themselves are rooted in social, not individual phenomena. The aggregate rate of suicide in a given society then becomes a "phenomenon *sui generis,*" (p. 13) and these individual acts become pieces of a larger puzzle that lends itself to sociological research (Anleu, 1995). Durkheim (1951) believed that societies, at given points in their history, have the capacity for suicide, and this would be measured by comparing the number of "voluntary deaths" (p. 48) to the overall population of that community. This may account for the capacity toward SbC that has been evidenced by

Western societies in a surge of completed and attempted suicides over the past several decades.

In discussing suicide, Durkheim (1951) posits that the action resulting in one's own death can be viewed as "a positive, violent action involving some muscular energy," (p. 42) or it may be "a purely negative attitude or mere abstention," (p. 42) such as the case of a hunger strike (1951). What differentiates the positive and negative action from a natural or accidental death, according to Durkheim, would be the cognitive state of the person regarding the mortality of such an action/inaction. Furthermore, Durkheim does not subscribe to the notion or belief that suicides in general are a direct or indirect form of insanity or mental disease, and he characterizes suicidal actors as distinguishable from general society only by their manner of death.

As previously stated, Durkheim's work was a foundation for future considerations on anomie (Merton, 1968)[6] and suicide. Such was the case with Merton's work on anomie in 1938 that was an expansion of Durkheim's original theory (Wallace, 2000). Merton acknowledged the contributions of Durkheim and others, such as Marx, Weber, Simmel, Pareto, Sumner, Cooley, and others as having provided vital material that helped shape future thinking on a variety of sociological issues including suicide (Merton, 1968).

Although Merton acknowledges the contributions and accomplishments of Durkheim on a variety of topics his discussions related to suicide are not as elaborate. In examining the theory of anomie advanced by Durkheim, Merton, according to McCaghy, Capron and

---

[6] Merton notes (1968:189) in Footnote #6 that the term anomie was believed to originate in the late sixteenth century by Joseph Glanville and was re-introduced by Durkheim.

Jamieson (2000), extends anomie beyond suicide as posited by Durkheim to include all

forms of deviance. Merton's theory is commonly referred to as *strain theory*, and according

to McCaghy et al., (2000) the primary differentiation between the theories are as follows:

- Durkheim believed that the aspirations of people are limitless and that rapid social change within a society will exceed what can be viewed as reasonable expectations.

- Merton argued that these same aspirations, although products of society, are limited. However, the aspirations may be obtained through unacceptable means.

- Durkheim believed that anomie was a result of a disruption of societal regulation that translated into a failure to maintain acceptable limitations.

- Merton on the other hand suggests that anomie is the result of strain in the social structure that in turn exerts pressure on individuals. The result of this strain is unrealistic aspirations on the part of the individual.

According to Merton:

"The cultural emphasis placed upon certain goals varies independently of the degree of emphasis upon institutional means. There may develop a disproportionate, at times, a virtually exclusive, stress upon the value of specific goals, involving comparatively little concern with the institutionally prescribed means of striving toward these goals. (Merton, 1968, p.187)

Unlike Durkheim, Merton provides alternative behaviors (McCaghy et al., 2000) or

adaptations (Wallace, 2000) to the experience associated with anomie. Merton identifies

the adaptations in the following model found in *Social Theory and Social Structure* (1968

p.194):

26

Table 1: Merton's Typology of Modes of Individual Adaptation

Modes of Adaptation	Culture Goals	Institutional Means
I. Conformity	+	+
II. Innovation	+	-
III. Ritualism	-	+
IV. Retreatism	-	-
V. Rebellion	±	±

Source: Merton, R. K. (1968). Social Theory and Social Structure. New York, The Free Press. P.194.

In discussing the typology shown in Table 1, Merton offers the following explanations:

- *Conformity* is present within a society that is considered stable. The social order of that society is sustained through a structured adherence to societal values and normative behavior. Deviance in this modality would not be common. (p. 195)

- *Innovation* maintains the emphasis on achieving cultural goals, but there exists an imbalance in the internalization of the societal norms for achieving these goals by acceptable institutional means. Deviance can occur when the institutionalized means are of an illegitimate nature, and Merton discusses "white-collar crime" in these terms. (Pp. 195-203)

- *Ritualism* is present when individuals have forsaken or minimized cultural goals that place a significant emphasis on status and success without jeopardizing personal values in adhering to the accepted institutional means. Merton cautions that this mode of adaptation is not necessarily deviant behavior, rather a deviation from cultural norms. (Pp. 203-207)

- *Retreatism* occurs with the least amount of frequency in individuals in comparison to the other modes of adaptation. Merton identifies individuals in this mode as living within a society, yet apart from it. Examples used by Merton in describing individuals that fit this mode are "outcasts, vagrants, vagabonds, tramps, chronic drunkards and drug addicts" (p. 207). Here there is a total rejection of normative goals and institutional means, and this form of adaptation is clearly deviant by societal standards. (Pp. 207-209)

- *Rebellion* is an adaptation that seeks a modification of the existing social structure that occurs when individuals encounter barriers to what are believed to be legitimate goals. Merton identifies rebellion in terms of an organized response by individuals seeking to impact on the *status quo*. (p. 209-211)

Not without criticism (McCaghy et al., 2000), Merton's theory is challenged for making certain broad assumptions on the representativeness of deviance within a given society. Although it may be argued that there is a disproportionate representation of "delinquency, crime, alcoholism, illegal drug use, and serious mental disorder" (p. 62) in the lower socio-economic classes, the official statistics initially relied on by researchers, including Merton, to make these assertions may be flawed.

Additional criticism (McCaghy et al., 2000) questions Merton's "assumptions of common goals and institutionalized means" (p. 63) that would not easily fit within the culturally diverse society of the United States. The cultural pluralism found in America and similar Westernized countries today may well overshadow formally homogenous goals.

II. Suicide-by-Cop

As previously noted, the literature on suicide-by-cop (SbC) is nominal and is only recently receiving more attention, and the interests in this regard extend well beyond the law enforcement community and minimally include the medical (Klinger, 2001) and legal communities. The term itself, without benefit of explanation, can be confusing. The ambiguity that can arise is not with the word suicide, but rather the reference to the word *cop* as shorthand for police officer may lead some to misinterpret the term to describe the suicide of a police officer. This jargon, although not ambiguous, does not clearly differentiate the role of the police officer in the suicide drama (Kennedy, Homant, and

Hupp, 1998; Luna, 2002).

The references found throughout the literature, for the most part, identify this suicide drama

as SbC. However, there are some differences, the majority of which are variations of the

"first formal definition of suicide by cop offered by Geberth" (Homant and Kennedy, 2000)

that can be found in *Practical Homicide Investigation,* 3rd Ed (Geberth, 1993). Among the

more commonly used terms that were found in the literature are "officer assisted suicide,"

(Geberth, 1993, p. 105; Keram and Farrell, 2001) and "police-assisted suicide," and

"hetero-suicide" (Mohandie and Meloy, 2000, p. 384). The term SbC, according to

Homant, Kennedy, and Hupp (2000), is advantageous, and presumably more preferable to

the authors in that the implication would be an officer's deadly force response is an

instrumentality of the suicidal actor. Katz (1998) criticizes the use of the term "assisted

suicide" and sees it as an oxymoron that is very misleading and inconsistent.

There are sufficient references throughout the literature as previously noted that attribute

the development of a formal definition for SbC to Vernon Geberth (1993). On the surface,

there appears to be little mention of the phenomenon prior to Geberth's discussion on the

subject. However, it was ten years earlier, in 1983, that a medical examiner in the county of

Los Angles, Dr. Karl B. Harris, began reviewing the deaths of persons who had been shot

by police in what appeared to be "deliberate provocation" [7](Rickgarn, 2001, p. 678) of

police officers (Homant, Kennedy, and Hupp, 2000). Dr. Harris is credited (Homant,

---

[7] In discussing provocation in this sense, Karmen (2004) differentiates between provocation and precipitation. The former, according to Karmen, is when an actor in an incident is the first to initiate the confrontation. Karmen views precipitation occurring when a person calls attention to himself or herself. This differentiation is critical in defining SbC and will be discussed in detail in Chapter 4.

Kennedy, and Hupp, 2000; Grella, 2000) as having been the person responsible for creating the term. An article in the *San Diego Union-Trib* (Brooks, 1991) "Suicide-by-cop is a growing problem in San Diego" (Homant, Kennedy, and Hupp, 2000, p. 44) is believed to be the first printed reference to the newly identified phenomenon of SbC.

Wolfgang's Victim-Precipitated Homicide

Aside from the limited definitional and historical references to Durkheim's study on suicide (Grella, 2000; Parent, 1998; Parent, 2004) the focus of the literature in identifying a starting point with this phenomenon begins with repeated references to the work conducted by Marvin Wolfgang (1958) in his classical study of homicide in Philadelphia (Grella, 2000; Homant, Kennedy, and Hupp, 2000; Keram and Farrell, 2001; Klinger, 2001; Lindsay, 2001; Luna, 2002; Miller, 2002; Parent,[1] 1998; Parent,[2] 2001; Parent,[3] 2004; Wilson, Davis, Bloom, Batten, and Kamara, 1998). It is from this study that Wolfgang classifies a particular type of death as being "victim-precipitated" (Wolfgang, 1958, p. 252).

Wolfgang (1975) defines victim-precipitated as:

> ". . . those criminal homicides in which the victim is a direct, positive precipitator in the crime. The role of the victim is characterized by his having been the first in the homicide drama to use physical force directed against his subsequent slayer. The victim-precipitated cases are those in which the victim was the first to show and use a deadly weapon, to strike a blow in an altercation—in short, the first to commence the interplay of resort to physical violence" (p. 252).

The Pre-Cursor to Victim-Precipitated Homicide

The basis for Wolfgang's definition of victim-precipitation (VP) originates with an analysis of theories focusing on social interaction, particularly the work of von Hentig. Here Wolfgang credits von Hentig's work in *The Criminal and His Victim* (1948) as providing

30

"the most useful theoretical basis for the present analysis of the victim-offender relationship" (p. 245). The victim-offender relationship in situations where violence has occurred between the two, from the view of von Hentig, is a very complex issue, and von Hentig does not allow for the victim to be considered without fault in the "evildoer—evil-sufferer" relationship (Jacoby, 1994. p. 32). According to von Hentig (1979), this relationship goes beyond the mere mechanics of a crime, with a victim and offender, and cannot be measured.

In discussing this further, von Hentig states:

> "If a study were to be made of a majority of persons victimized by the same criminal, using the same method, in the same circumstances, science would gain a more comprehensive picture of this subject-object relationship, which has not only theoretical but practical significance. Most crimes leave us with an unknown lawbreaker and a known victim. A thorough knowledge of all possible and typical relationships between the one who injures and the one who is injured presents the investigator with valuable clues, as do the mode of execution, the locality of the crime, and the time it was committed" (von Hentig, 1979, p.387).

The inability to measure the underlying subjective nature of this doer-suffer relationship is still evident today. Perhaps it is for this reason that there is no clear understanding of why a person will provoke or force another to use force to the point of causing the death of the initial aggressor such as in the case of SbC.

In his analysis of von Hentig, Wolfgang clearly notes[8] that von Hentig asserts that there are incidences wherein a victim of a murder may have intentionally caused their own death at the hands of another, and von Hentig classifies these victims by "psychological type" (p. 246). For whatever reason Wolfgang admittedly does not incorporate "von Hentig's

---

[8] The notation can be found in Wolfgang's (1958) *Patterns in Criminal Homicide* in Footnote 2 found on page 246.

psychological types" (p. 246) into the 1948 – 1952 Philadelphia study. Wolfgang's initial

omission of this typology from the original analysis of Philadelphia study should not be

overlooked, and it is not until he followed up *Patterns in Criminal Homicide* with a journal

article that appeared in the *Journal of Clinical and Experimental Psychopathology*

reporting on a follow-up analysis of the data did he discuss the possibility that the actions

of a person in victim-precipitated violence may result in suicide (Klinger, 2001).

Suicide as Victim-Precipitated Homicide

Following the release of *Patterns in Criminal Homicide*, Wolfgang acknowledges that

serendipity[9] (1961, p. 335) led him to further analyze the data from the Philadelphia study

since the original data "yielded a fortuitous by-product, an unexpected observation" (p.

335). This by-product, not anticipated in the original hypothesis, was the observance that

some VPH cases may involve deaths that could be categorized as suicide.

The initial study of VPH by Wolfgang in the Philadelphia study closely examined the

precipitating actions of the victim. To better understand the dynamics of this violent drama

Wolfgang synthesizes examples of individual cases examined in the Philadelphia study in

the following vignettes:

- A husband accused his wife of giving money to another man, and while she was making breakfast, he attacked her with a milk bottle, then a brick, and finally a piece of concrete. Having had a butcher knife in hand, she stabbed him during the fight.

- A husband threatened to kill his wife on several occasions. In this instance, he attacked her with a pair of scissors, dropped them, and grabbed a butcher knife

---

[9] Wolfgang discusses the matter of serendipity as being an experience that is fairly common, and results in the observance of an anomaly, often times resulting in the development of a new hypothesis and further research.

32

from the kitchen. In the ensuing struggle that ended in their bed, he fell on the knife.

- In an argument over a business transaction, the victim first fired several shots at his adversary, who in turn fatally returned the fire.

- The victim was the aggressor in a fight, having struck his enemy several times. Friends tried to interfere, but the victim persisted. Finally, the offender retaliated with blows, causing the victim to fall and hit his head on the sidewalk, as a result of which he died.

- During a lovers' quarrel, the male (victim) hit his mistress and threw a can of kerosene at her. She retaliated by throwing the liquid on him, and then tossed a lighted match in his direction. He died from the burns (Wolfgang, 1975, p. 253).

The "interdependent relationship between victim and offender" (Grella, 2000, p. 4) has

long been the nexus between Wolfgang's theories on victim-precipitated homicide.

However, there is something that is missing in the work in *Patterns in Criminal Homicide*

(1958) and *Suicide by Means of Victim-Precipitated Homicide* (1961).

Wolfgang summarizes the analysis of the Philadelphia study as follows:

> "In many cases the victim has most of the characteristics of an offender: in some cases two potential offenders come together in a homicide situation and it is probably only chance which results in one becoming a victim and the other an offender. At any rate, connotations of a victim as a weak and passive individual, seeking to withdraw from an assaultive situation, and of an offender as a brutal, strong, and overly aggressive person seeking out his victim, are not always correct. Societal attitudes are generally positive toward the victim and negative toward the offender, who is often feared as a violent and dangerous threat to others. However, data in the present study—especially that of previous arrest record—mitigate, destroy, or reverse these connotations of victim-offender roles in one out of every four criminal homicides." (1961, p. 335)

There is no mention in this passage, or even an inference that Wolfgang entertained the

thought that these cases of VPH involved an intended suicide by a person using the police[10]

as a mechanism, and there is only a passing reference, one sentence, in the article that refers

---

[10] Fyfe (2004) notes that between 1950-1959 police-related homicides in Philadelphia were relatively rare with 29 reported cases, and this data would not support a statistical analysis such as the homicide study.

to the involvement of the authorities in these acts. Wolfgang (1975) notes: "In some cases he may actually kill in order to receive punishment and expiation at the hands of the authorities." (p. 342) This reference to expiation is not elaborated on, and it is not clear if Wolfgang is describing a situation wherein a person expects instantaneous expiation or punishment to be delivered through the legal system.

In light of the extended gap between the work of Wolfgang in the late 1950s and the initial writings on SbC that emerged in the early 1990s, research on this topic that has been recently produced has proved to be invaluable and thought provoking. The research and studies that were reviewed for this research relied on a variety of data found in official records, through secondary analysis, and by content analysis of incidents that have occurred in the United States and Canada in the last twenty or so years.

One of the earlier studies focusing on SbC resulted from the analysis of 437 officer-involved shootings in the Los Angeles County Sheriff's Department occurring between 1987 and 1997 (Honig, 2001; Bresler, Scalora, Elbogen, and Moore, 2003). This study conducted by Hutson, Anglin, Yarbrough, Hardaway, Russel, Strote, et al. (1998) determined that 10.5 % of the shootings could be classified as SbC. This percentage remains the baseline reference in the majority of the literature on SbC (Allen, 2004; Grella, 2000; Homant, Kennedy, Hupp, 2000; Homant and Kennedy, 2000; Homant and Kennedy, 2001; Lord, 2000; Lord, 2004: Parent, 1996, Parent, 2001; Parent, 2004; Paynter, 2000; Roberts, 2001).

Connecting Victim-Precipitation and SbC

Of the many researchers and authors that have written on SbC with proficiency and a great

deal of regularity (Homant, Kennedy, Hupp, 2000; Homant and Kennedy, 2000; Homant

and Kennedy, 2001; Lord, 2000; Lord, 2004), Parent's (1996) examination of deadly force

incidents in British Columbia that were categorized as SbC was among the first. In

researching the "underlying reasons for police use of force" (iii) Parent examined the

situational nature inherent in policing, particularly violent encounters resulting in a deadly

force response by officers.

In focusing on Wolfgang's principle of victim-precipitated homicide (VPH), and Wolfgang

and Ferracuti's (1967) theory on the subculture of violence, Parent (1996) was able to place

the SbC incident into perspective. Citing Geberth's (1993) anecdotal research on SbC,

Parent relates the suicidal actions of a person engaging an officer in a deadly force

encounter as analogous to Wolfgang's VPH by asserting that VPH "is in *essence* (emphasis

added) a form of suicide" (p. 4). However, it could be argued that this generalization of

VPH by Parent as being a form of suicide is not completely accurate. If a person, bent on

self-destruction, purposely aims a weapon at a police officer with the expectation of a

deadly force response by that officer is then shot and killed by that officer, then that

person's action(s) precipitated his or her own death. Conversely, if a person engages in

behavior that results in his or her own death it would not be axiomatic that the person

expected or intended to die as a result of their actions. Therefore, a valid criticism of the

use of victim-precipitation as a generalization in SbC incidents can be made. It does not

accurately describe the drama for the purpose of examining SbC incidents. In Wolfgang's

earlier work it was evident that death was not always an intended or expected outcome in victim-precipitation as would be the case in a SbC incident. The actions of the suicidal actor in this sense are initiating the deadly force confrontation and the intended outcomes are much clearer.

As one of the earlier published academic works on SbC, Parent's 1992 thesis may well have planted the seed for the relative frequency of many researchers in connecting Wolfgang's VPH and SbC. Parent's position and reliance on VPH as a way of classifying SbC is well directed. However, it will be presented further in this paper that the actions of the a person in this suicidal drama are scripted for the purpose of committing suicide and a more appropriate classification would be *victim-scripted suicide*. Initiation of action with a desired outcome of death will more likely involve a decision, either overt or subliminal, on the part of the suicidal actor, and this decision will be the outcome or result of previously scripted behavior or thought.

The initial research conducted by Parent (1996), which serves as the source of repeated secondary analysis in subsequent publications (Parent, 1998; Parent, 2001; Parent, 2004), examines the role of victims in situations where the use of deadly force occurs, or the likelihood of its use is very high. Parent conducts his analysis of identified incidents in the context of the lawful use of force by police officers as dictated by Canadian Provincial Law and existing departmental policies. The incidents identified for possible analysis are found in agency records of the Police Commission in British Columbia, as well as vital statistics of the provincial coroner.

Parent synthesizes the many theoretical perspectives presented in examinations of the reasons why police can and will resort to the use of force, specifically deadly force. The result of his synthesis is a categorization of seven perspectives. These perspectives according to Parent are predictors, physiological changes, stressors, individual characteristics, variable relationships, victimology, and theories of violence (p. 38). The first four of these perspectives, predictors, physiological changes, stressors, and individual characteristics all share certain elements, and should be viewed as highly fluid in the sense that these variables will most certainly never be the same in any given incident. In discussing predictors, Parent notes that participant attributes, of the actor(s) and officer(s), "are key factors in determining the use of deadly force" (p. 38), as are environmental factors, motivational factors of actor(s) and officer(s), and other perceptions of the officer(s) at the scene. The same attributes of the actor(s) and/or officer(s) found in the predictors of deadly force will be occurring simultaneously with the physiological changes and stressors that are experienced by the actor(s) and/or the officer(s), and these responses are a direct result of the individual characteristics of the parties involved.

Parent (1996) examined shootings in British Columbia that occurred between the period of 1980 and 1994. The research "focused upon categories of resolution utilized by police to incapacitate a perceived deadly threat" (p. 64). Parent relied on data found in "police reports and government documents (p.64)" that included the *B.C. Police Commission Annual Report On Shots Fired By Police Within British Columbia*, records that were used in consideration for valor awards for police officers, and reports from the B.C. Coroner's office. This focus resulted in what Parent identifies as "four . . . independent sources of information" (p. 73) that are as follows:

1. *B.C. Police Commission's Annual Report On Shots Fired By Police.*

2. *B.C. Commission's – "Police Honuors Night" official records.*

3. *B.C. Police Department Records, Investigations and Interviews.*

4. *C.C. Coroner's Office – "Verdict-At-Coroner's Inquest" reports.* (1996, p. 73)

Initially, Parent reviewed 45 files that fit the research criteria that he had established. These criteria sought police files that reported on incidents involving the use of deadly force by officers resulting in death, or incidents involving the use of deadly force by police, but death of the subject did not occur. Parent determined that approximately 45 % (n= 20) of the original files would not fit the criteria he had operationalized, and he eliminated them from the analysis. Acknowledging that the initial database would be nominal, Parent supported his research with interviews (p. 81) of many of the police officers that had been involved in shootings that fell within the operationalization of the study. In some cases, the exact number was not identified, or the incident occurred over 10 years prior to the start of the research that created a logistical problem of locating surviving officers. In those cases where the officer, or the file, could not be physically located, the file was excluded. Another cause for exclusion of a file would be incidents wherein the actions of the officer, although involving deadly force, would not have resulted in serious bodily injury or death of the subject. An example given by Parent would be in the case of an officer firing at a fleeing felon in a motor vehicle and "it was extremely unlikely that wounding or death would have occurred as a result of the police officer's discharge of a firearm" (p. 76). A third identified factor that caused the file to be excluded from analysis was the vagueness of the police file. The final reason given by Parent for excluding a case file was due to an overload of information in the file that made it difficult, if not impossible; to determine what actually had happened without conjecture. Parent had labeled these files "cluster files" (p.76).

The types of shootings that Parent examined in the remaining twenty-five files included:

- The utilization of deadly force by discharging a firearm;

- The utilization of deadly force that did not result in death; or

- Incidents involving a resolution without the use of deadly force wherein the officer would have been legally justified in the use of deadly force (p. 64).

In considering these shootings, Parent was also interested in issues as they related to certain characteristics that existed prior to, during, and after the incident as they related to the officers involved. These characteristics included:

- Individual characteristics of the officers involved;[11]

- The age, length of service, and assignment of officers;

- Situational and perceived stressors during the incident;

- Training on less-than-lethal[12] options;

- Situational factors; and

- The degree of critical incident stress affecting the officer (p. 65).

Parent initially examined a total of "45 files" (p. 76) that potentially fit the criteria that involved incidents of persons having been shot by police in British Columbia for his analysis. He had determined that "at least 30 individuals were killed by police" (p. 74)

---

[11] In reviewing the cited Appendixes, C and D that are noted on page 65, it could not be determined what is meant by individual characteristics. An analysis of Appendix C reveals questions regarding the preparedness of the officer. This section inquires of the type of training the officer had received regarding the use of deadly force, and the subjective determination of the officer if that training had prepared them for a deadly force encounter.

[12] Options in this regard are presently categorized as *less lethal* recognizing that the application of less lethal options still present the possibility of lethality when used.

during a 14-year period from 1980-1994. The total (N=30) incorporated incidents involving

municipal police (n=15) as well as the Royal Canadian Mounted Police (RCMP) (n=15). In

examining data relative to the wounding of persons by the RCMP or municipal police

officers Parent identified the lack of standardization in reporting these incidents by the

RCMP in comparison to the local authorities. Parent discovered at the time of his research

that the RCMP does not provide this information, delineating incidents involving the

wounding of a person or suspect by RCMP personnel, to the B.C. Police Commission (p.

75). The municipal authorities on the other hand reported a total of 15 individuals who

were identified as "non-police personnel" (p. 75) as having been wounded over a period of

15 years. Additionally, the municipal authorities reported "13 separate incidents" (p. 75)

where officers had used deadly force, but did not wound the individual.

In reviewing the files pertaining to the *Police Honours Night*, Parent identified a total of 21

files, RCMP (n= 12) and municipal police (n=9) (p. 78). The total number of files for

analysis amounted to 34, of which 25 were obtained from the *Shots Fired* data and nine

from the *Police Honours* data (p. 81).

The last data analysis conducted by Parent in his research was on reports detailing the use

of deadly force by the police that were compiled through the *Verdict-At-Coroners-Inquest*

(p. 83). In seeking data for the period of January 1980 through January 1995 Parent

discovered that the Coroner's office was only able to provide information that could be

considered "accurate" (p. 83) for the period of time between January 1989 and January

1995.

In all, Parent examined 58 cases, 34 involving municipal police officers and 24 involving

the RCMP, wherein the officers had been confronted with a perceived lethal threat. Of the

total (N=58), Parent found that in 27 incidents the police officers used deadly force

resulting in the death of 28 people. Of the 31 cases remaining it was determined that the

officers relied on less lethal force to resolve the incident (p. 86). From these cases Parent

asserts that victim-precipitation is responsible for the actions of some of the individuals

who had confronted the police, thereby causing their own death at the hands of the police.

What is not clear from the findings and interpretations of Parent's research is what

percentage accurately represents victim-precipitated homicide as operationalized in the

research, or could any of the shootings have involved something other than victim-

precipitation?

In discussing characteristics of the individuals involved Parent reports that in over half of

the cases examined the deceased had consumed a "significant" amount of alcohol or drugs

prior to death with a "high level of impairment" (p. 96). The percentage of blood alcohol or

the presence of particular narcotics is not mentioned. Similarly, the discussion relative to

mental illness and irrational behavior is equally less informative and reports that "roughly

half" of the study population exhibited these characteristics. Finally, Parent reports that

approximately 28 % of the cases involved individuals who exhibited irrational or bizarre

behavior and that these individuals had "engaged the police in a life-threatening manner,

prior to being shot and killed" (p. 97).

Overall, Parent raises several salient, thought-provoking and interesting points regarding

the actions of individuals in provoking a deadly force response by police officers. Although his sample is taken from police files of agencies in Canada, the similarities between police

agencies from the United States and their neighbors to the north should allow for the

generalizations made by Parent. However, this particular research by Parent does not lend

itself to allow for generalization of SbC.

The Medical View of SbC

Wilson, Davis, Bloom, Batten, and Kamara (1998)[13] conducted a study of the deaths of 15

persons who had been characterized as suicidal. Specifically, it was the manner of death of

these persons that had generated interest in the medical field. The authors note that there

were discrepancies in the determination of the manner of death by different pathologists in

three separate cases in the Portland, Oregon area in the 1990s. According to Wilson et al.

the medical literature on the "suicide by provocation of police" (p.46) was nominal, and

they noted the need for mental health professionals to gain a better understanding of

suicidal persons who opt to use provocation of the police as a mechanism for death.

The Wilson et al. (1998) study focused on cases wherein the "case investigation must have

identified, with reasonable probability, that the victim provoked a police officer to shoot at

the victim and the victim had suicidal ideation or intent" (p. 46). Excluded from the

analysis were cases where the victims, according to Wilson et al. were suffering from acute

cocaine intoxication. The researchers note that cocaine psychosis "may confound" (p. 46)

the persons ability to form suicidal intent. The method for identifying the presence of

---

[13] Edward F. Wilson, M.D. is listed as a deputy medical examiner for the State of Oregon. Joseph H. Davis, M.D. was the former chief medical examiner, Dade County, Florida. Joseph D. Bloom, M.D. is listed as the Dean of the Medical School, Oregon Health Sciences University, Portland, OR. Peter J. Batten, M.D. is a former medical examiner in Marion County, Oregon, and listed with the Department of Psychiatry, Oregon Health Sciences University, Dr.. Skeku G. Kamara, Ph.D. is listed as member of the research faculty, The Washington Institute, University of Washington, Tacoma, WA. This information is contained in footnotes 1-5 of the article submitted by Wilson et al., (1998).

cocaine within the system was toxicological tests that would have been performed during the autopsies of the deceased suicidal actor.

The analysis was descriptive in nature and relied on 21 variables that were used to determine the classification of death. Of the 15 cases examined eight had occurred in four counties in Oregon with the remaining seven having occurred in Dade County, Florida (1998, p. 48). The variables were categorized into groups. The groups were identified as personal information, criminal behavior, dangerous behavior, toxicological data, mental illness, and death certification data.

The results of the analysis on personal information revealed that the vast majority of the subjects were male (n=14), and Whites (n=13) far outnumbered the one Black and one Hispanic, both of whom died in Florida. The authors reported that the ages ranged from 17-61 years, and that the mean was 32 years. All of the subjects (N=15) were categorized as having resisted arrest, and the majority (n=11) was armed with firearms, 10 with handguns, and one with a handgun as well as a rifle. Toxicological tests performed at the autopsy revealed that there was evidence of alcohol in six of the decedents with the minimal blood alcohol level as measured in grams at .10 %, and the highest concentration .22 %. The number of subjects that threatened suicide (n=10), had recently completed suicide notes (n=8), and had previously attempted suicide (n=8), although nominal, will be used as a premise for further analysis to be conducted in the present study. This will be discussed further in the chapter on methodology.

A final note on the analysis of the data by Wilson et al. (1998) revealed that there was "excellent documentation" that in one-third of the cases (n=5) there was severe mental illness (p. 47). The illnesses in these cases were identified as Major Depression, chronic alcohol abuse, Atypical Psychosis, and Bipolar Disorder (formerly termed Manic-Depressive Illness) (p. 47). There was only one case identified that manifested co-morbidity and involved the diagnosis of Major Depressive Disorder and chronic alcohol abuse. In the remaining cases (n=10), the evidence of psychiatric illness was compelling (Pp. 47-48). Two of the cases evidenced substance abuse by the decedent, one case revealed that the decedent manifested Paranoia and Chronic Depression, another chronic depressive had a previous suicide attempt, another chronic depressive abused multiple substances, one case was a mentally retarded male in his 20s who had a previous suicide attempt, there were two chronic depressives who also abused alcohol, and finally two cases of Chronic Depression.

It was also discovered that in all (N=15) of the cases the investigation subsequent to the death determined that the decedent intended to die at the hands of the police by provoking a deadly force response by the police. The police reports, statements of witnesses, as well as family and friends of the decedent reportedly verify this. This factor coupled with the preceding data demonstrating a possible correlation between communicating suicidal ideation and the act of committing suicide-by-cop (SbC) will be the foundation for the postulate that suicidal persons who contemplate SbC will most likely communicate this to a person(s) that is within their familial or social structure, or directly to the police.

Overall the authors found that the "provocation" of police into using deadly force (1998, p. 50) accounted for a relatively small amount of justifiable homicides. Additionally, they noted that at the time they conducted their research there was little in the way of medical or forensic literature that examined the topic of the provocation of police into using deadly force.

In identifying the paucity of literature on the subject, Wilson et al. (1998) recommend that considerations be given by the medical-legal communities to establishing more accurate criteria for the classification of deaths resulting from the use of deadly force by the police. Durkheim (1951) questioned this very point when he asked, "Shall suicide be considered to exist only if the act resulting in death was performed by the victim to achieve this result" (p. 43)?

Determining percentages in SbC Incidents

A study conducted by Kennedy, Homant, and Hupp (1998) examined "hidden suicide" (p. 23) that they felt was illustrative of the insidious nature of SbC incidents. The researchers were interested in determining whether SbC accounted for "some meaningful percentage" (1998, p. 23) of police shootings, and if SbC incidents involved any discernible identifiers that would separate them from police shootings that occur under more traditional circumstances.

To obtain data for their research, Kennedy et al. (1998) examined news stories from 22 newspapers covering 18 metropolitan areas. The parameters of the research were based on police shootings between January 1980 and June 1995, which resulted in 887 articles meeting the criteria. A total of 240 separate incidents were identified as suitable for study.

The data was analyzed by what the authors describe as "Two experienced police officers with master's degrees in criminal justice[14]" (p. 23). These officers then rated the incidents independent of each other. The rating of the incidents was gauged by five categories: Probable Suicide; Possible Suicide; Uncertain; Suicide Improbable; and, No Suicidal Evidence. The two categories that help establish the foundation for SbC are probable and possible suicide. In cases rated as probable suicide the researchers identified what is characterized as "clear suicidal motivation, either by word or gesture or they confront the police with a dangerous weapon despite having no way to escape, virtually forcing the officers to shoot" (p. 24). A subject who has the appearance of being disturbed or "otherwise act as if they do not care whether officers kill them" (p. 24) characterizes the second category, possible suicide. The possible suicide may make a vain attempt to escape the violent actions of the police, which were in response to the initial provocation.

The demographic variables that were evident in the data examined revealed that the subjects in the vast majority of the cases, 97 %, were male. Sixty-eight percent of the subjects ranged in age from 16 to 35, and mental illness or homelessness was evident in 5 % of the cases.

Kennedy, Hommant, and Hupp (1998) acknowledged that the initial findings were vague in identifying suicidal motivation in any of the shootings with a range from 16 - 46 %. A cross-validation study was conducted as a follow-up to the original analysis. In the follow-up study the authors took a new sample of news stories reported in the *Detroit Free Press* for a period of one year from 1992 to 1993. The results of the follow-up study were similar,

---

[14] The authors fail to clarify further as to what other credentials these experienced officers have other than length of service time and graduate degrees.

with 47 % of the incidents having the possibility of suicidal motivation. Again, the authors acknowledge the vagueness of the results, but argue that these results help support the conclusion that SbC is not a rare occurrence.

Following the 1998 study, Homant, Kennedy, and Hupp (2000) examined 123 SbC incidents that resulted in death or were in some way averted. The researchers examined the level of dangerousness that was involved in the incident and then checked the level of dangerousness against other variables present during the incident. The 123 cases were complied from the literature that was available at that time, along with media accounts of SbC incidents, case law analysis, Internet sources, and a local police department. The authors were of the opinion that the behavior of the suicidal actor in the SbC drama was not typical, and they were interested in identifying the variations in the hopes of identifying a typology of the cases that had been researched up until that point.

In citing Hutson et al. (1998) and Lord (1998), Homant and Kennedy (2000) note the variations in the situational variables that have been found in SbC, such as incidents evolving from domestic violence, mental illness, a history of suicidal ideation or behavior, histories of alcohol and/or substance abuse, or a desire to escape from future incarceration. This earlier research was establishing a foundation that demonstrated early on that these incidents could originate as the result of various circumstances. Furthermore, SbC incidents were characterized as either planned or unplanned, and according to Lord, as cited by Homant and Kennedy (2000), the majority of the cases involving SbC were spontaneous. The spontaneity of these incidents is of considerable concern and will be discussed further in this research.

In defining SbC Homant and Kennedy (2000) identified an SbC as involving a person, who by virtue of his or her behavior, acted in a manner that seemingly was intended to provoke a law enforcement officer(s) to use deadly force, specifically by shooting the person. Threats to harm a third party by the suicidal actor were also a consideration along with the communication of suicidal intent such as in the leaving of a suicide note. More importantly, they excluded incidents in which, although the actions of the actor may have the appearance of a desperate person, such as in a shootout with police during a criminal incident or escape from custody, without additional indicators could not be related to suicidal intent.

In their analysis of the data, Homant, et al. (2000) categorized SbC incidents into three categories. The categories differentiated between confrontation and intervention, and the categories were then divided into types. The first category was identified as *Direct Confrontation*. The direct confrontation is described as an incident wherein the actor consciously plans an attack on the police. A total of 30.8 % of the cases (n=44) were categorized as being of this type. The direct confrontation was sub-categorized by the type of attack, sudden or controlled. The sudden type of attack, or *Kamikaze attack* (p. 344) accounted for 3.5 % of the incidents (n=5) generally involved a surprise attack on police officers or fixed posts such as a police station or precinct. The second type of attack was categorized as being controlled in that there is no direct attack against police; rather the actor confronts the police in a threatening manner with some type of deadly weapon resulting in a deadly force response. This type of attack was found in six cases (4.2 %). A third type of attack involved the manipulation of the police into responding to and/or investigating a crime or violation. The manipulation of a police response occurred in 15.4

% of the cases (n=22). The fourth and final type of attack was categorized as being

dangerous in that the actor deliberately manipulates the police into a confrontation.

Examples of these types of attacks included hostage situations or the commission of a

serious crime with the apparent full expectation of a police response. A total of 7.7 %

(n=11) fell into this category.

The second of the three broad categories, *Disturbed Intervention*, accounted for 57.3 % of

the SbC cases (n=82). As the term implies this category involves individuals whose

behavior is often times described as irrational or emotionally disturbed. The person in these

cases may manifest suicidal behavior or "seize" (p. 346) the moment with suicidal

ideations. The three sub-categories involve the intervention of a suicidal person, the

domestic violence incident that produces an actor who views suicide as the only option to

an otherwise hopeless situation, or the actor who is disturbed due to intoxication from

drugs or alcohol and mental illness.

In the incidents involving an intervention by the police of a potentially suicidal person, the

researchers found that 20.3 % (n=29) of the cases met the established criteria. The cases

that were categorized as *Disturbed domestic* occurred 16.8 % of the time (n=24).

In examining the occurrence of SbC as a result of conflict arising from relationship

problems Homant, et al. (2000) highlight a case study based on information gleaned from a

newspaper article.[15] The case example used by the researchers detailed the ending of a

relationship between a 17 year old, who was learning disabled, and his girlfriend. After a

failed suicide attempt, wherein he was hospitalized and later released, the young man,

---

[15] The article appeared in the *Denver Post*, May 4, 1995.

armed with a replica handgun, entered a supermarket where the young woman worked. In the ensuing incident the young man pointed the replica handgun at a man and his daughter. As a result of his actions he was shot and killed by police. The conclusion that is made in a case such as this is that the young man was not capable of coping with the ending of the relationship by the young woman. Therefore, he may have rationalized that his life was, and would continue to be, useless without the companionship of his girlfriend. The selection of the mechanism, in this case SbC, is not clearly identified. Why did the young man choose SbC, or an equally as important and perplexing question: Did he?

The third sub-category, *Disturbed person*, was found to account for 20.3 % of the cases (n=29). The actor in this type of SbC drama may be intoxicated, under the influence of drugs, suffering from some form of mental illness or emotional problem. Homant, et al. (2000) note that there may be evidence of previous suicidal thoughts or attempts by the actor, and the actions of the actor in the present case indicate that the actor prefers death at the hands of the police.

The final general category of SbC behavior, according to Homant, et al. (2000), occurs during police intervention at a crime in progress. The researchers discovered that 11.9 % (n=17) of the incidents involved the commission of a crime, where the police, resulting in SbC, unexpectedly interrupt the criminal actor. In these cases the actors were not willing to be apprehended for their criminal activities, and death was an acceptable alternative, or they may well have been willing to accept the consequences of a high-stakes gamble.

The sub-categories of *criminal intervention* included involvement in criminal activity, the nature of which spans from minor to serious. In incidents involving the latter, serious crime, the actor has made a personal commitment that does not include prison as an option. In incidents involving SbC arising from a minor criminal incident or offense Homant, et al. (2000) differentiate this type from serious or major crime in that the actor is opposed to police intervention on matters related to principle or ego. What begins as something that is relatively inconsequential, such as a motor vehicle violation or a simple assault, then escalates into a major confrontation between the police and the actor resulting in a SbC incident. This type of incident involves a degree of spontaneity wherein the actor in this particular violent drama acts consciously to "seize the opportunity" (p.348) of the police intervention. According to the authors the actor in this drama is "someone with underlying suicidal motivation" (p.348), and they found that 5.6 % (n=8) of the cases fit this category.

In evaluating the typology that they have created, Homant, et al. (2000) established a series of points to test for exclusivity and exhaustiveness. First, they had to determine if the incident fit the broad category of SbC. The second point was established if the actor's decision in this drama was determined to be a planned event. If the event was categorized as having been planned it was identified as a Category I. Other incidents that did not show evidence of having been planned were categorized as II or III. A Category II incident would involve an actor who had exhibited "some sort of disturbed behavior" (p.349), and the Category III actor would have been involved in a criminal matter that would not have been considered to be extraordinary.[16]

Once having categorized the overall typology Homant, et al. (2000) then evaluated the 174 incidents placing them into one of three categories. The researchers then compared the

---

[16] The authors are describing criminal behavior that in everyday human activity is considered normal or ordinary. The authors are not normalizing the activity itself, rather the frequency of occurrence in day-to-day activities.

results of their analysis to that of a third independent rater as a measure of rater reliability. The level of agreement between the researchers and the independent rater that the generalized classification of the incidents fit that of SbC was 96.5 % with a reliability coefficient (Φ) of 0.87. Further comparison on agreement of the categorizations that had been made by Homant, et al. (2000) with that of the independent rater dropped to 78 %; Φ= 0.74, and in the comparison of the nine types there was agreement in 60 % of the cases; Φ = 0.58[2] (p. 350).

In identifying the lack of agreement of the categorizations Homant, et al. (2000) attributed this to the subjectivity of the rater and the researchers in determining the motivation of the suicidal actor. Additionally, they acknowledged that the detail in the scenarios that were reviewed might have been so complex that there is the possibility that more than one interpretation could be made by independent raters.

Homant, et al. (2000) acknowledges certain weaknesses in their study. They note that the low number of cases in the types they have identified does not allow for sufficient generalization. They also believe that although the cases they examined are "reasonably representative" (p. 353) of SbC, there is a good possibility that the sources may over represent the phenomenon. A final self-criticism of their study points to what they believe may be a weakness in their methodology. They note that the "findings on rater reliability and validity are based on the same sample of incidents from which the typology was derived" (p. 353).

Hutson, Anglin, Yarbrough, Hardaway, Russel, Strote, Canter, and Blum (1998) focused

on officer-involved shootings that were investigated by the Los Angeles County Sheriff's

Department between 1987 and 1997 (N=437). The cases examined by Hutson et. al.

(n=46) met four criteria:

- There was evidence of suicidal intent;

- There was evidence that the person wanted the police to shoot him or her;

- There was evidence of the possession of a deadly weapon or something that represented one; and/or

- There was evidence that the person intentionally escalated the encounter provoking the officer(s) to use deadly force.

The researchers determined, based on the established criteria, that 11 % of the shootings

occurring during the 10 year period were SbC incidents, and these shootings accounted for

13 % of the justifiable homicides involving police officers in that jurisdiction. Additionally,

the study revealed that the majority of actors were male (98%), the ages ranged from 18 -

54 years and that 48 % of the weapons used were firearms. A smaller percentage (17)

involved some form of replica firearm (Hutson et. al., 1998).

Motivation and Indicators of SbC

An analysis of SbC by Mohandie[17] and Meloy[18] (2000) examined the phenomenon by

focusing on the clinical and forensic indicators found in seven case studies. Their analysis

of SbC focuses on three separate, but related factors. They discuss the range of motivations

found in SbC cases as well as presenting certain risk factors and indicators that are found in

---

[17] A police psychologist employed by the Los Angeles Police Department.

[18] An associate clinical professor of psychiatry, University of California, San Diego.

incidents of suicide and violence. Finally, they describe what are considered to be specific

indicators found in SbC incidents.

In discussing motivation relative to suicide, Mohandie and Meloy (2000) unequivocally

state that suicidal behavior is goal-directed. According to the authors, in some cases the

goals would either be instrumental or expressive. An instrumental goal may emerge in the

form of avoidance of consequences arising from the actor's actions. A person who has

established that incarceration is not an option or one who has failed to reconcile a

relationship would fit these criteria. The person who is depressed, hopeless, or expressing

rage exemplifies expressive goals.

In detailing the instrumental category Mohandie and Meloy (2000) posit that individuals in

SbC incidents may seek to escape or avoid the consequences of their actions that were

criminal and/or reprehensible. The actor may use a confrontation with police as the result

of a failed relationship. In light of clauses in insurance policies that prohibit claims from

being filed resulting from suicidal action, the actor may stage a police confrontation. SbC

can relieve a person from the religious stigma associated with suicide. A final motivation

for resorting to SbC is the belief that the means will ensure the end.

Conversely, the authors note that expressive goals arise as a form of communication. The

individual can be experiencing a sense of "hopelessness, depression, and desperation" (p.

385). The actor may view himself or herself as a victim in the true sense of the word, and

the actions of the police, resulting in death, truly exemplify this. Surrender is not an option.

The actor's need for power may be overwhelming. Rage or revenge could be a factor. A final consideration would be the actor's "need to draw attention to an important personal issue" (p. 385).

The differences between instrumental and expressive motivations in SbC, according to Mohandie and Meloy (2000), are shown in Table 2. The verbalizations in this table are taken from actual cases involving attempted or successful SbC incidents.

TABLE 2: Instrumental versus expressive motivations in suicide by cop.

Instrumental	Expressive
"I'm not going back to jail"	"My life is hopeless"
"I wanted her to come back to me"	"I am the ultimate victim"
"God won't forgive me if I do it, but He will if you do"	"Soldiers never surrender"
"Make sure my kids get the insurance money"	"I am important enough to be killed by the cops"
"I can't do it myself"	"I'll teach you a lesson"
	"This is worth dying for"

(Mohandie, J.R. and Meloy, R.K. (2000). Clinical and Forensic Indicators of "Suicide by Cop". *Journal of Forensic Science*, 45(2), 384-389.

Reporting on studies conducted by Shneidman (1996), Mohandie and Meloy (2000) note that 90 % of cases of completed suicide involve some form of verbal or behavioral clue demonstrated by the suicidal actor in the week preceding the act. However, Shneidman notes that in cases involving threatened suicide the majority of the cases do not result in an attempt or completed act. This finding, according to Shneidman, mirrors similar research on violent behavior that has found that the threat to commit violence does not necessarily result in the attempt or completion of a violent act.

Mohandie and Meloy (2000) identify 10 types of verbal clues common to suicide in the general sense. The following is a generalization of these verbal clues: They may be considered direct or veiled threats. Statements of hopelessness, self-hate, or intense guilt are also common. There may be statements made identifying depression, emotional and/or physical pain, or statements that might suggest identification with a person(s) who has attempted or committed suicide. Finally, statements may be made in the form of *verbal wills* or irrational thoughts or obsessions (p. 388).

The behavioral clues associated with general suicidal behavior according to Mohandie and Meloy (2000) might include a clearly violent act toward the self or others. An obviously reckless or careless act that clearly places a person in danger would be another indicator. The active use of controlled substances or alcohol in excess of acceptable or prescribed norms, or conversely abstaining from necessary medications or treatments necessary for sustaining some quality of life are also indicative of behavioral clues.

Overall, in their analysis of SbC, Mohandie and Meloy (2000) have revealed that careful examination of the history of the actor in a SbC incident may reveal sufficient verbal and behavioral clues that could have warned of potential risk factors in this regard. Additionally, the present circumstances involving the actor, as in the case of a person who is hopeless, depressed, suicidal, and/or refusing to be held accountable for his or her actions, may be useful in understanding what the actor's "motivation and intent" (p. 388) could be.

In incidences of SbC the behavioral and verbal clues noted by Mohandie and Meloy (2000) is for the most part quite obvious and in many ways these clues are overt in nature and intent. Indicators of verbal clues that may be evident in SbC would be the actor demanding that the police kill him or her, at times a deadline for action may even be set by the actor. Other examples cited by the researchers include the actor verbalizing their will or desire to die, identifying with the glory associated with a gun battle with police, clearly emphasizing that incarceration is not an option, or by referencing Biblical or religious verses.

Similarly, the behavioral clues exhibited by a person acting in a provocative manner that would most likely be construed as leading toward SbC are at times quite overt. The pointing of a weapon, particularly firearms, in the direction of police, or as in some cases the actual firing of the weapon is often a sure means of achieving a desired end. However, in instances involving the taking of hostages wherein the actor delivers ultimatums or begins a countdown intended to force the police into action it may not be as clear at the onset of the actor's intentions, but subsequent investigation, information, and analysis reveal the SbC intent. Another behavioral method that can ensure a particular police response would be self-mutilation in the presence of the police. This behavior would most likely trigger an initial police response that is intended more as a life saving consideration. The tragic twist in this type of scenario would be for the actor to attack officers as they closed any gap in proximity resulting in a self-defense posture by the police.

Law Enforcement Assisted Suicide
In an analysis of 64 cases of SbC, Lord (2000) found that there were detectible differences in the characteristics of persons who were successful in their attempts to force a police officer to use deadly force and those who were not. Lord examined cases from 32 law enforcement agencies throughout North Carolina that occurred during the 1990s. In a review of the literature, the author notes that the literature focusing on SbC prior to this point was sparse. According to Lord, one possible reason for the lack of academic research in this regard may be due to the perception of some, particularly suicidologists, that the relatively small number of cases identified as SbC does merit extensive analysis. Lord

57

discounts a position such as this as flawed in the sense that SbC may be more prevalent than what is presently accounted for.

Lord (2000) defines SbC in a manner similar to Mohandie and Meloy (2000) relying on the presence of verbal or behavioral clues that upon further analysis can reveal the actor's intent. However, in referring to SbC as *law enforcement-assisted suicide*, Lord is clouding the problems of classification mentioned earlier in this paper.

An SbC is considered to be successful, according to Lord (2000), if as a result of their actions the SbC actor provokes a law enforcement response of deadly force that causes death or injury to the actor. Additionally, Lord includes incidents involving suicide by the actor during the course of the SbC incident as also being a successful incident. Lord did not categorize those cases that were resolved without injury or death, such as in the case of a surrender or similar conclusion, as successful.

The data analyzed by Lord (2000) originated with local and county law enforcement agencies located throughout North Carolina, and involved incidents that occurred between 1991 and 1998. With a defined classification of SbC, Lord interviewed police personnel in these various agencies who were assigned to tactical or negotiation units and elicited their perspective of the incidents. All interviews by Lord were supported with an extensive review of the case histories[19] and evidence, as well as supporting documentation found in accounts of family and witnesses.

---

[19] Lord notes that although there was some variation in the type of information from department to department, the records maintained by these agencies were for the most part very detailed. According to Lord this is attributable to the fact that the incident involved the use of force by police.

Recognizing that the majority of the variables examined were nominal, Lord (2000) in examining the measure of association, relied on lambda (λ) using a cross-tab analysis in an attempt to detect if there was any relationship between outcome and variables associated with the personal and situational characteristics found in an SbC incident (p. 406).

In analyzing the 64 cases Lord (2000) used a frequency analysis in describing the demographic variables of the SbC actor. Overall, males far outnumbered (n=61) females (n=3), and involved whites (n=48) more often than African Americans (n=14). The highest percentage in age was found to occur between the ages of 25 - 39 (n=36). Almost one-half (n= 30) of the incidents resulted in the actor being injured (n=9) or killed (n=16) by the police, or suicide (n=5).

In comparing the personal and social characteristics of the SbC actor Lord (2000) categorized the outcome of the SbC incident as successful versus unsuccessful. The independent variables developed to compare the personal and social characteristics are generalized as mental disorder, substance abuse, social isolation, stability in maintaining residence, and work history.

In examining the relationship of mental disorder Lord (2000) found that the majority of cases (n=29) the actor was not believed to suffer from mental illness. A slightly higher margin of those who were not believed to be mentally ill (n=16) were successful in SbC. In those cases where the actor had a history of commitment (n=8) the success rate was higher than those who were identified as unsuccessful (n=6).

The examination of substance abuse was bifurcated by Lord (2000) separating incidents into cases involving a history of substance abuse (n=52) and cases involving substance abuse occurring during the incident (n=57). Both of these variables included absence of abuse, alcohol, prescription drugs, marijuana, alcohol and marijuana, hard drugs, and alcohol and hard drugs.[20] An analysis of these results revealed that the use of hard drugs (n=10) slightly eclipsed alcohol (n=9) in cases involving abuse exclusive of the SbC incident. However, the abuse of alcohol by actors in SbC incidents (n=32) far exceeded the use of other substances or combinations of substances.

In so far as the impact of social isolation and the ability to maintain stability of a residence, Lord (2000) discovered that there was a weak relationship between the lack of familial support and SbC, and that the incidence of SbC more frequently involved actors who had shown evidence of maintaining a stable residence for more than one year (n=41). Of interest in this is the observation that those identified as not having a residence (n=5) were much more likely to be successful in their intent. The reasoning offered, although empirical, is that a person who is not familiar to the police officer may be perceived to be more of a threat than a person who the officer has some sort of relationship with. The dangerous flip side to decision making based on familiarity is that sound tactical judgment of a police officer in a life and death situation can be clouded to a point that may result in deadly mistakes.

---

[20] Lord (2000) identifies cocaine as one type of hard drug. This would be problematic in that cocaine is not readily identified with suicidal behavior as noted by Wilson, Davis, Bloom, Batten, and Kamara (1998). Perhaps a more definitive list of drugs/narcotics in this area should be offered.

The final variable examined by Lord (2000) in this area related to the employment history

of the subject. It was found that in those cases where the employment history was known[21]

(n=45) more than half of the actors were unemployed (n=28).

Another comparison examined by Lord (2000) related to what could be categorized as a

stressful life event of the SbC actor. Again, this variable was compared to the outcome of

successful or unsuccessful SbC. Stressful life events, in those cases where it could be

identified (n=56),[22] focused on the ending of relationships (n=19), family problems (n=12),

financial difficulties (n=3), mental illness (n=10), criminal (n=6), having a combination of

problems (n=6), or cases where no problem was determined or present (n=7).

Problems associated with the ending of a relationship were found to be present in the

majority of the cases (n=19), and that those who were unsuccessful (n=10) in SbC were

narrowly higher than those who were successful (n=9). Family problems closely followed

the former (n=12) and again the unsuccessful (n=7) were slightly higher in number than the

successful SbC (n=5).

In comparing suicidal ideation and prior suicide attempts to outcome Lord (2000) found

that the majority of the former (n=31) had shown or revealed some evidence of ideation.

However, it was found that in the majority of the latter there was no evidence of a previous

suicide attempt (n=37). In regards to any evidence of planning the SbC incident it was

found that the successful and unsuccessful SbC incidents were evenly split (n=32). The

---

[21] Lord (2000) had noted that the although the cases often were extensive in the amount of information
contained, the missing information may be attributable to the lack of standardization in reporting by the
various police departments in the study.

[22] Not all cases included sufficient information to determine stressful life events (n=63).

weapon of choice of the SbC actor in slightly more than 74 % of the incidents (n=47) was some type of firearm. The successful SbC incidents involving firearms (n=28) were significantly higher than those that were unsuccessful (n=19).

The final comparison focused on indicators of aggression and anger of the SbC actor. The variables in this comparison included criminal history, the initial role of the police officer, and verbalization of the SbC actor. The vast majority of cases involved actors with no criminal history (n=31).[23] The most common type of offense in this comparison involved some form of domestic violence (n=11).

The analysis of the role of the police officer is perhaps the weakest area in an otherwise persuasive study of SbC. Considering that the SbC incident involves two primary players, the SbC actor and a police officer(s), this is the only area of the study to focus on the police. The majority of the time the initial role of the police officer is suicide intervention (n=26) followed by domestic violence (n=20) or criminal activity (n=17). An interesting result in this comparison was the number of successful incidents involving criminal activity (n=12) that exceeded suicide intervention (n=9) and domestic violence (n=9), both of which had higher rates of unsuccessful SbC with suicide intervention (n=17) exceeding domestic violence (n=11). The rate of unsuccessful SbC incidents involving suicide intervention (n=17) almost doubles the number of successful incidents (n=9). These results could lead to speculation that the majority of persons involved in these incidents did not actually want to die and some intervening variable may account for the unsuccessful outcome.

---

[23] Data was missing for this analysis and the total number of cases analyzed was N=61.

Lastly, Lord (2000) examines the verbalization of the SbC actor. The vast majority of the

cases (n=37) involved some form of direct verbalization by the actor with 13 being

successful, and almost double that number (n=24) was not. Similarly, in incidents involving

verbalizations associated with homicide and suicide, as would be the case of a person

threatening to kill a police officer or another third party along with himself or herself,

successful SbC incidents (n=9) are more than double unsuccessful incidents (n=4).

Overall, Lord's (2000) analysis of the 64 cases of SbC incidents that occurred over a period

of eight years (1991 – 1998) revealed that the characteristics found in some SbC actors and

the general population who commit suicide have certain commonalities, and share similar

risk factors.

A Uniform Reporting Mechanism: A Two-Tiered Approach
In their examination of SbC, Pinizzotto, Davis, and Miller (2005) focus on the lack of a

uniform definition, and recommend the need to develop a national uniform reporting

mechanism in line with the Uniform Crime Reporting (UCR) Program to accurately

capture SbC incidents. The authors have collectively researched the use of deadly force

involving law enforcement officers for over 15 years (2005, p. 10). During the course of

this research Pinnizzotto et al. have examined cases that were indicative of SbC. However,

they note the lack of a uniformed definition of SbC has proved problematic in accurately

categorizing SbC and attempted SbC incidents.

Pinizzotto et al. (2005) define SbC as "an act motivated in whole or in part by the

offender's desire to commit suicide that results in a justifiable homicide by a law

enforcement officer" (p. 10). This definition emphasizes the motivation of the suicidal actor

63

as being a significant factor in determining if the incident meets necessary criteria for

classifying an incident SbC. Additionally, the authors recommend that attempted SbC

incidents be similarly defined and evaluated in an effort to "better understand the

magnitude of the suicide-by-cop phenomenon" (p.10).

In an attempt to better understand and account for SbC Pinizzotto et al. (2005) suggest the

use of the UCR Program as a vehicle for collecting information relative to SbC. Citing the

1990 expansion of the UCR to include data collection on hate crimes, Pinnizotto et al.

suggest a similar expansion of the UCR that includes a two-tiered investigative procedure

that would thoroughly investigate police-involved shootings that are believed to be SbC

incidents. The first level or tier in the investigative procedure would be the basic

preliminary report submitted by the law enforcement officer on the scene of an SbC

including statements made by the actor and/or others, pre-incident actions of the actor, and

circumstances that would indicate suicide as a motivator. This phase would require that the

officer involved in the SbC make a determination as to the motive of the actor. The second

level or tier would be a follow-up to the preliminary report and would serves as a

classification of the incident by an investigator with expertise in matters related to the use

of deadly force. This follow-up investigation would delve into information not readily

available to the officer completing the initial investigation. It is here that Pinnizotto et al.

identify items and facts that may lead an independent, objective evaluator in reaching a

conclusion that the incident was an SbC. These items and facts may include

communication of intent, corroborating statements from family, friends, co-workers or witnesses, and other supporting evidence[24] that could substantiate a classification of an incident as SbC.

The recommendations of Pinnizotto et al. (2005) raise two concerns; one is definitional, the other procedural. The lack of an objective standard within the definition to determine motivation leaves the definition incomplete. Without basic guidance police officers may well be left to their own inductive reasoning in attempting to determine motivation, and the subjectivity of each officer will play a critical role in this regard. The second concern is with the recommendation that motivation of the actor be included in the preliminary report that is to be filed by the investigating police officer. This recommendation suggests that the preliminary investigation goes beyond reporting the facts of the case requiring them to form an opinion.

The first concern will be addressed through the development of a definition of SbC that allows for an objective determination of motivation/intent of the suicidal actor. The second concern will be addressed with recommendations made in the conclusion of this report.

Script Theory

Script theory has its origins in psychology and is applied by cognitive psychologists to define a "mental representation" (Dwyer, Graesser, Hopkinson, and Lupfer, 1990) of the actions or activities that a person would or could be expected to "enact frequently or in a conventional manner" (p. 296). Abelson (1981) describes the script as "embodying knowledge of stereotype event sequences" (p.715). Scripts exist in understanding as well as in behavior, and when a person enters a script there is usually a commitment by that person

---

[24] Pinnizzotto, Davis, and Miller (2005, p. 12) note the availability of mobile video recorders currently used by many law enforcement agencies as one potential source for corroborating evidence.

to complete or finish the script thereby creating what Abelson identifies as an "action rule" (p. 719).

The premise in script theory is an emphasis on goals, plans, and actions in organizing knowledge (Dywer, et al., 1990). A second element of script theory entails "investigations of expertise" (p.300). Dwyer, et al. have constructed their research in such a way that recognizes a level of expertise in the understanding and application of the use of deadly force by police officers.

Dwyer, et al. (1990) cite Abelson (1981) in identifying three necessary conditions required for scripted behavior to occur: "(1) the person must have a stable cognitive representation of the particular script; (2) an evoking context for the script must be self-presented or environmentally presented; and (3) the person must physically enter the script" (Dwyer, et al., 1990. p.296). The first condition, having a stable cognitive representation of the particular script, is not as complicated as it may sound. If a person, in this case a police officer, is exposed to an incident, event, or similar stimuli and comes away from that exposure with the knowledge of how people or things are expected to act/react under similar circumstances, it would be logical to assert that police officer is building the foundation for a stable cognitive representation of that incident. Repeated exposure and subsequent reinforcement under similar circumstances can be expected to then reinforce the police officers cognitive understanding and representation of that script. The same would then hold true for people in other professions as well as in the general population, and this scripted behavior may in fact lead to a form of shorthand that is trigged by an anticipation to a set of circumstances that then leads to a scripted response.

Research conducted by Dwyer, et al. (1990) was intended to determine if script theory

could be applied to an analysis of decisions made by law enforcement officers in situations

dealing with the use of deadly force. Police officers, according to Dwyer, et al. develop

scripts based on stereotypical situations, that are rooted in experience and training. The

stereotypes in these situations are not to be confused with the negative image of

stereotyping. To the contrary, a police officer who has observed a person committing a

crime may note specific mannerisms associated with that particular crime. A good example

would be the officer who has observed a narcotics transaction and specifically detects a

hand-to-hand transaction involving money and an unidentifiable object. This observation

would be supported by training in the area of narcotics investigation and perhaps previous

observations of this nature. Based on the script theory posited by Dwyer, et al. the officer in

the preceding example would formulate a script related to narcotics transactions that would

be "internalized" (1990. p.297), and similar behavior observed by the officer would be

viewed in accordance with the previously developed script.

The script(s) developed by police officers is not a knee-jerk reaction to an unfamiliar

situation, and these incidents do not occur in a vacuum. The script is based on a frame of

reference that the officer has added to his or her individual repertoire. This frame of

reference, or script, allows the officer to form "expectations and to make inferences about

the potential outcome of a set of events" (Dwyer, et al. 1990. p. 296). Officers will develop

a variety of scripts as they learn and advance through their career. The response of the

officer is then affected as the incident unfolds and variations on the expectations of

behavior are changed. From a practical standpoint, the development of scripts by police

officers would be advantageous so long as the responses of the officers are in accordance with the appropriate laws, policies, and procedures. However, the obvious negative implications associated with this theory may occur if the script(s) that have been developed are based on prejudices, improper or erroneous training, or faulty interpretations of the observations and experiences of the officer(s). In such cases the response of the officer(s) would be less than optimal and may in fact be contrary to generally acceptable practices.

Dwyer, et al. (1990) examine the utility of applying script theory to the decision making process involved in deadly force situations, as well as to whether the decisions made by officers under these circumstances had been affected or influenced by training in the application and understanding of the use of deadly force. The study was conducted in the aftermath of the United States Supreme Court decision, *Tennessee v. Garner* (1985), that significantly affected the way in which police officers applied deadly force. The *Garner* decision prompted a paradigm shift away from the previously acceptable "fleeing felon" rule which allowed police officers to use deadly force to stop a fleeing felon from escaping apprehension, regardless of the threat that that person posed, to a much more restrictive application of deadly force. Under *Garner*, the officer must now assess the dangerousness of the situation, in a narrow time frame, as to whether their life or the life of a third party is in danger. This shift in policy and procedure required a re-thinking of the use of deadly force policies across the Nation. It is within this post-*Garner* era that Dwyer, et al. looked to test the viability of the script theory as it applies to the application of deadly force by police officers.

The study focused on two main questions; (1) how police officers are trained to make judgments in deadly force situations; and (2) what cognitive strategies are used under the new guidelines by individual officers in these situations (Dwyer, et al. 1990. p. 295).

The researchers identified two major categories of scripts that were determined to be "directly relevant" (Dwyer, et al. 1990. p. 296) to the use of deadly force by a police officer. The first script was the *social situation* script and the social situation script was a part of the officer's long-term memory. Social situation scripts are associated with the vast number of incidents that a police officer may be likely to encounter in their day-to-day activities. The majority of the social situation scripts identified by Dwyer, et al. focused on criminal activity such as theft of a motor vehicle, domestic violence, gang-related activities, and robbery. There are countless numbers of other social situation scripts that are stored in the officer's memory, and although these incidents may not directly involve deadly force decision-making, script theory recognized these social situation scripts as being a critical component of a deadly force script.

Dwyer, et al. (1990) tested their theory on the application of script theory to the decision making process involved in the use of deadly force by police officers using a controlled experiment. The researchers constructed a survey instrument consisting of 61 crime scenarios that were based on actual incidents. The scenarios were followed by a series of options (4) intended to measure the respondent's choice based on their interpretation of the scenario. The respondent was then asked to give a justification as to why he or she selected a particular course of action. Table 3 illustrates an example of a scenario followed by the options.

The survey instrument was distributed to 142 sheriff's deputies from a county sheriff's office in Shelby County, Tennessee. The respondents comprised the ranks of sheriff's officer, sergeant and lieutenant, all of whom had been trained under the new guidelines associated with *Garner.* Participation in the survey was voluntary and occurred during the department's annual In-service training.

Table 3: An Example Scenario

While driving through the city park at midnight, you and your partner hear yelling coming from a wooded area. You both get out to investigate and about 40 feet away you see a female on the ground with a male astride her. They are struggling. Although it is rather dark, he has what appears to be a hunting knife in his had.
You would:

1. Not draw your weapon
2. Draw
3. Aim
4. Shoot
Why?
(Source: Dwyer, et al. (1990). *Application of Script Theory to Police Officer's Use of Deadly Force.* Journal of Police Science and Administration. Vol. 17, No.4, p. 297.

The analysis of the data collected revealed that the respondents similarly rated scenarios 71 % of the time, and the remaining 29 % varied on the decision to use deadly force. An overwhelming majority of the respondents, 95 %, were in agreement in the decision to draw their weapon, and of that percentage, 90 % had selected the aiming of the weapon as an option, with 33 % of that group opting to use deadly force. Additional analysis of difference in decisions between ranks was found not to be significant.

Dwyer, et al. (1990) found that overall the responses to the scenarios by all of the officers were "very consistent" (p. 300). The noted differences in decisions were based on whether the respondent had decided to use deadly force are illustrated in Table 4.

Dwyer, et al. (1990) performed multiple regression analyses on the data in an attempt to assess the predictability the scenarios may have on the respondent's decisions regarding the use of deadly force. In developing the multiple regression equation the researchers included cumulative proportion scores. The scores bifurcated respondents into a proportion of those who would draw, aim, or shoot in contrast to those who decided to aim or shoot.

It was reported, as shown in Table 5, that the "most informative" (p. 299) of the regression analysis were those that involved "the criterion variable of shooting the suspect(s)" (p.299). The equation in this analysis was found to be significant ($p < .05$) for both nonsupervisory, with 51 % variance, and supervisory officers, with 50 % variance.

Table 4: Proportion of Responses by Rank

Response	Nonsupervisory (N=81)	Supervisory (N=61)
(N) No Draw	.08	.04
(D) Draw	.11	.10
(A) Aim	.54	.59
(S) Shoot	.27	.28

(Source: Dwyer, et al. (1990). *Application of Script Theory to Police Officer's Use of Deadly Force*. Journal of Police Science and Administration. Vol. 17, No.4, p. 299.

Table 5: *Beta* Weights or Predictors

Factor	Nonsupervisory	Supervisory
Suspect has weapon	.51*	.49*
Suspect intends to harm	.33*	.37*
Suspect is committing felony	.29*	.27*
Suspect is leaving building	.24*	.23*
Variance Predicted (R^2)	.51*	.50*

(Source: Dwyer, et al. (1990). *Application of Script Theory to Police Officer's Use of Deadly Force*. Journal of Police Science and Administration. Vol. 17, No.4, p. 300.

Dwyer, et al. (1990) found the utility of the application of script theory to the decision-making process involving the use of deadly force by police officers provided an unique approach to examining this process, and to further the knowledge in "one of the most critical areas of law enforcement" (p. 301).

This research will expand the utility of the work on scripted behavior by Dwyer et al. (1990) by applying the principles of script theory in SbC incidents where it can be determined that provocation of police in SbC occurs in a sequence of cause and effect actions.

CHAPTER 3

Suicide-by-cop (SbC) is in need of a deeper analysis that will allow for an exploration

of the phenomenon in an effort to identify variables that have not been identified in the

literature as of yet (Creswell, 1998; Marshall and Rossman, 1989). An exploratory

qualitative analysis of specific SbC case studies can allow for a micro-level analysis of

how police practitioners perceive and understand SbC as well as examining the

dynamics of the incident (Denzin and Lincoln, 2003), specifically the actions and

reactions of the suicidal actor toward police.

The qualitative approach to study SbC incidents offers the ability to portray the incident

in a natural setting without scientific alteration (Creswell, 1998), and further offers the

ability to build in the necessary flexibility that is crucial to qualitative research

(Marshall and Rossman, 1989). The interests driving this research lie with the general

phenomenon of suicide-by-cop in regards to evidence of intent vis-à-vis communication

by the suicidal actor, and the actions of the actor in entering the suicidal drama.

However, to better understand the phenomenon it is necessary to delve into these

individual cases simultaneously (Denzin and Lincoln, 2003) in an attempt to determine

if there is the possibility that the data can produce results that are capable of

generalization.

The literature review has helped to formalize the research design and methodology for the

present study on SbC and scripted behavior in the SbC drama. This was done by

establishing a baseline of information relative to demographic and situational variables that

have been previously identified as being present or existing in SbC incidents. The review of

73

the literature has shown that there is consistency in the demographic variables of the SbC actor. The majority of actors are males (Bresler, Scalora, Elbogen, and Moore, 2003; Brubaker, 2002; Hutson, Anglin, Yarbrough, Hardaway, Russel, Strote, Canter, and Blum, 1998; Honig, 2001; Kennedy, Homant, and Hupp, 1998; Lord, 2000; Lord, 2004; Luna, 2002) who range in age from their mid-twenties to their mid-fifties (Bresler, Scalora, Elbogen, and Moore, 2003; Brubaker, 2002; Hutson, Anglin, Yarbrough, Hardaway, Russel, Strote, Canter, and Blum, 1998; Honig, 2001; Kennedy, Homant, and Hupp, 1998; Lord, 2000; Lord, 2004; Luna, 2002). Family and personal relationship problems will be found in the majority of cases, and in those cases where there is evidence of substance use/abuse (Bresler, Scalora, Elbogen, and Moore, 2003), the drug of choice will be alcohol in the majority of the cases (Honig, 2001; Hutson, 1998; Lord, 2000; Lord, 2004; Parent, 1996). However, what has not been consistent in the literature is the application of a standardized definition of what SbC is, or just as important, what it is not. Although there are similarities in the literature defining the phenomenon, a standardized definition has not yet emerged, and it is this lack of clarity that will account for a considerable number of SbC incidents being misclassified by practitioners and academics alike.

The central question to a study such as this (Creswell, 1998) is: Can a conceptualization of the phenomenon of suicide-by-cop be developed from a practitioner's perspective? Using the case studies supplied by the FBI, this research will review each case in an effort to determine what factors, variables, or research led the submitting officer to conclude that the case was SbC. The resulting analysis of these cases will result in the development of a conceptual model of how SbC is understood by the cohort responsible for conducting the original case studies. Assuming that sufficient information can be extracted from the files a

74

model will be constructed that will reveal how the phenomenon is perceived by police practitioners'.

A subordinate question to the more general central question would be: Is the type or kind of aggressive action used to provoke a police officer(s) into resorting to a deadly force response scripted?

An affirmative answer to either of these questions will help to support the utility of this particular research. An implication of this, obviously, is that careful analysis of any such scripts identified in the research might aid officers to quickly identify just what they are involved in, and to develop intervention strategies that might interrupt the scripts and avoid the outcome – death – intended by the suicidal actor.

Based on the central and subordinate questions that are the foundation for this research, it is believed that SbC can be clearly defined, and that scripted behavior of the suicidal actor can be identified. In those cases that reveal a preponderance of facts that support a classification of SbC as established in the methodology developed for this research it will be necessary to examine the actions of the suicidal actor in a step-by-step analysis. Therefore, it becomes necessary to examine SbC incidents in a micro-analysis that goes deeper than current macro-level analysis that have served the necessary function of identifying frequency distributions of situational and demographic variables found in SbC incidents. The general literature on suicide refutes a common misperception held by many, that suicidal individuals do not verbalize their intentions. Verbalization of aggression or suicidal intent related to a provocation of the police will be found in the data more commonly than might be expected. Furthermore, it will be shown that the behavior of suicidal actors in many of these case files can be categorized as scripted, and this scripted

behavior will be considered *victim-scripted suicide*.

This research is a secondary analysis of individual case studies of police files of incidents

that have been categorized as fitting the generalized criteria that classify an incident as

being SbC. The FBI collected the case studies (N=61) over the course of several years.

The data set consists of various police department's case files on police-involved shootings.

The range of information found in a preliminary review of the files include reports

submitted by the officer(s) involved, supplemental reports submitted by the officer(s),

supervisors, investigative personnel, medical records, personal history of the person killed

by the police, news clippings, internal investigative reports, and medical examiner's

reports. The exploratory nature of this research accounts for the anticipated variation in

how cases originate, the variances in police policy and procedure, the differences that will

be found in investigative style, and the lack of standardization in each of these areas.

The underlying interests driving this research center on the utility of the study and the

knowledge that can be gained and shared in the interest of identification, prevention, and

minimizing victim-scripted suicide. Toward this end, it is critical to identify the line of

inquiry that will be pursued when examining the data.

One of the questions addressed by this research focuses on whether or not pre-planning of

an SbC incident by a suicidal actor has the elements associated with scripted theory.

Accepting that scripted behavior is based on a "cognitive structure" (Dwyer, et al., 1990, p.

296) that activates in "stereotypical situations, allowing the person to have expectations and

to make inferences about the potential outcome of a set of events" (p. 296) allows this research to proceed with the inquiry into the probability that SbC incidents involve a level of scripted behavior based on individual characteristics of the suicidal actor as well as situational variables preceding the drama and as it unfolds.

Dwyer, et al. (1990) applied script theory to their analysis of the decision-making process of police officers as it related to deadly force. This research model was considered a good fit by Dwyer, et al., citing Gentner and Jezioski (1989), in noting that expert scientists make decisions "based on relationships between components in a system rather than surface properties of isolated components" (Dwyer, et al. 1990. p. 300). It is the position of Dwyer, et al. that the police officer is relying on expertise when making decisions related to the use of deadly force, and that the "decision to shoot is based on deriving the intentions of suspects" (p. 300) and what plans related to the commission of crime by the suspect become known to the officer.

For the purpose of this research it will be posited that a majority of individuals involved in SbC incidents will act with a generalized social understanding, the cognitive structure (Dwyer et al., 1990), and an expectation, or stereotype (Abelson, 1981), of a police response to a deadly force situation. The actions of the suicidal actor in the SbC drama will proceed along lines directed by cause and effect. This incident will not occur in a vacuum, an each incident will present unique demographic and situational variables involving the suicidal actor and police.

Although this application does not meet the more rigid expectations of conventional script theory, the underlying principle of this research is rooted in the belief that the police response to deadly force situations is common knowledge and is evident in many facets of human coexistence in democratic societies. From the games played by young children, such as *cops and robbers*, the entertainment and news media that graphically, albeit frequently in an improper context, portray police practices, or personal experiences with police officers in use of force situations as demonstrated by police agencies; or as a result of a face-to-face encounter, involving a direct or indirect use of force, there exists a generalized consensus of what an appropriate and likely police response would be in a deadly force situation. Granted, this generalized consensus would not meet the rigorous standards of scientific understanding. However, if a person were to build upon the general consensus on appropriate police response by consciously, or subconsciously, focusing on ways to counter the police response, then it can be argued that that person is building a frame of reference. This frame of reference can then be the foundation for the first of the three elements, "a stable cognitive representation of the particular script", (Dwyer, et al., 1990, p. 296) required for script behavior to be considered. The second and third elements, self-presenting or environmentally presented, and physically entering the script should be readily identifiable in the SbC incident.

CHAPTER 4

This study is designed to conduct qualitative research on SbC that is exploratory in nature

(Creswell, 2003; Creswell, 1998) in an attempt to gain greater understanding of the

phenomenon (Denzin and Linclon, 2003). The lack of a formalized, standard definition of

suicide-by-cop, which is a socially constructed phenomenon, can lead to an erroneous

generalized view of the dynamics of SbC. The ability to rely on rich descriptions (Denzin

and Lincoln, 2003) of the individual cases found within the data set will help to crystallize

the understanding of SbC that is necessary for developing the foundation for meaningful

quantitative analysis.

In discussing qualitative inquiry, Creswell (1998) suggests that there are several compelling

reasons for undertaking this approach. The ability to describe *what* is occurring as opposed

to *why* is intrinsic to qualitative research. Second, there is the lack of established or tested

theories associated with the SbC drama. Third, greater understanding of SbC can occur

with the use of a qualitative approach such as the case study that is bounded temporally and

spatially. Fourth, the use of qualitative analysis allows for an examination in a natural

setting. The fifth, sixth, and seventh reasons Creswell suggests the use of qualitative

inquiry focus on the interests and limitations of the researcher. Writing style, available

resources, and audience are considerations that often solidify the selection of this approach.

An eighth, and final consideration, according to Creswell, for selecting a qualitative inquiry

is the ability of the researcher to emphasize his or her role as one who is learning from the

data in contrast to the "expert" (1998, p. 18) who is judgmental.

Qualitative research is inductive by nature proceeding from an examination of the particulars found within the case(s) moving to a broader, more generalized perspective (Creswell, 1998; Stake, 2003). Case study analysis allows the researcher to draw from facets bounded by the case as well as from other contextual factors that may impact on one or several cases under examination (Stake, 2003).

As previously noted, SbC is a socially constructed phenomenon that is particularly intriguing in light of a lack of a clear definition as to what constitutes SbC. To gain a necessary understanding of the phenomenon with the expectations of developing certain generalizations regarding the suicidal actors in incidences of SbC, this research will rely on a case study approach in examining the data.

The focus of the research determines the type of case study to be employed (Creswell, 1998). The three types of case study are *intrinsic, instrumental,* and *collective* (Creswell, 1998; Stake, 2003). If the focus of the study is on a specific case, perhaps due to the uniqueness of the case (Creswell, 1998), or there is a particular trait (Stake, 2003) found in that case then an intrinsic case study would be used. A second approach is to examine a particular case with an interest on the issue or issues associated with the case. The case in this approach is an instrumentality (Creswell, 1998), a means to an end, to better understand the area of interest. The third and final type of case study is the collective case study. This approach is used to study more than one case (Creswell, 1998) or a number of cases (Stake, 2003) involving a phenomenon (Stake, 2003) such as SbC. The collective case study approach is the proposed course for the analysis of the data in this research, and will consist of a review of all case files (N=61) by a single principal researcher. Each case file will be reviewed for completeness and suitability for analysis by a principal researcher.[25] Toward that end it will be necessary to determine if the case file contains sufficient information that extends beyond situational and demographic variables. The sufficiency of information will be viewed based on the existence of factors that are present in the case file that when examined objectively would result in a classification of SbC .

Operationalization

The selection of case study analysis for this research is based on the subject matter to be studied and is not considered a methodological choice (Stake, 2003). The phenomenon of suicide-by-cop is the primary interest, and the individual cases will be a mechanism to facilitate better understanding of the phenomenon in general. The cases contained in the data are expected to range from the simple to the complex (Stake, 2003). The case files, based on a preliminary random analysis, reveals that the extensiveness of the information contained in the files range from limited to robust.

Each case will be examined for inclusion or exclusion based on the existence of sufficient information that allows for a categorization of the case as fitting established criteria of the SbC incident. Purposeful sampling (Creswell, 1998; Creswell, 2003) allows the researcher to examine the case, or cases, in an attempt to gain greater understanding into the area of interest.

The criteria that will be used in this study to determine SbC classification are the following:

---

[25] The principal researcher is a twenty-five year veteran, command-level officer, with a large northeastern United States police department, and is qualified as an expert in the instruction and investigation of use of force incidents. This researcher has served as a supervising firearms instructor at the local, county and state level, and has been assigned as a senior internal affairs officer responsible for investigating cases involving police use of force.

- Evidence of suicidal ideation;

- Evidence of movements, gestures, or similar mannerisms provoking a response by the police officer(s) present;

- The use of replica or non-functional weapons;

- The use of functional weapons;

- Verbalizations or other communications associated with suicide; and/or

- Demanding or provoking a particular police response that is illogical under the circumstances.

The existence of demographic or situational variables that will result in not classifying a case SbC will include the following:

- Attempts at escape from apprehension;

- Incidents identified as occurring due to questionable police procedures that may have had a counter-effect resulting in a self-defense posture by the citizens involved;

- Incidents involving self-inflicted wounds;

- Incidents involving an authorized use of deadly force from commanding or supervising officers; and/or

- Evidence of mental illness, defect or obvious indicators of a lack of cognitive ability of the actor.

As noted in Chapter 3, a standardized definition of SbC has not yet emerged in the literature. In constructing such a definition there can be no room for ambiguity. In order to objectively define SbC there is a need to develop a litmus test that separates SbC from other police-involved shootings. The decisiveness of this approach focuses on the intent of the actor in the drama, and whether or not it can be determined if their actions were suicidal. Therefore, the litmus is the intent of the suicidal actor, and whether this intent can be clearly and objectively determined.

For the purpose of this research, SbC will be defined as: An incident involving the use of deadly force by a law enforcement agent(s) in response to the provocation of a threat/use of deadly force against the agent(s) or others by an actor who has voluntarily entered the suicidal drama and has communicated verbally or nonverbally the desire to commit suicide. The three elements of this definition will allow for an objective determination to be made in categorizing an incident SbC.

Scripted behavior relative to SbC will be defined as any behavior accompanied by some form of suicidal communication that is an obvious indicator of aggressive behavior on the part of the suicidal actor that provokes a response by the police officer. This response, initially, may cause the responding officer to assume a defensive posture, such as maintaining or seeking cover, withdrawing from the hostile area, or verbalizing commands intended and expected to stop the behavior of the actor. Behavior of the suicidal actor, that is offensive in nature, which then causes a change in response by the officer, will be categorized as scripted.

Data Processing

A preliminary review of the case studies reveals that decisions to submit a file to the data set was either speculative or preponderant on the part of the submitting officer. Speculative files have limited information and may only contain basic, preliminary police reports, follow-up investigative reports, and in some cases news clippings. These files lack sufficient synopsis or analysis of the case by the submitting officer, and in some cases contain no independent discussion of the case. Therefore, a complete reading of each of these cases in order to determine suitability for analysis for the purpose of this research was necessary.

Case files that fit the category of preponderant are extensive and robust compilations of police reports, statements, medical reports and/or diagnosis, and external determinations made by the submitting officer related to classification of the outcome of the incident as SbC. These files are expected to provide sufficient information in both a synopsis and analysis of the case by the submitting officer.

Regardless of how the file is classified, as speculative or preponderant, the proposed procedure for recording the data for analysis will be to adhere to a single protocol (Creswell, 2003). This protocol will consist of collecting notes on each case that has been determined to meet the specific criteria for inclusion while simultaneously collecting demographic data for use in conducting a limited frequency distribution analysis. Creswell recommends that the use of notes in qualitative research include descriptive as well as reflective entries. Descriptive notes or entries, according to Creswell, are intended to allow the researcher the ability to describe participants in the study, to reconstruct dialogue, describe the milieu, and to account for particular events or activities. Reflective notes allow the researcher to record personal thoughts, and for this study will be used to record thoughts as to why the submitting officer has reached the conclusion classifying the case as SbC, if in fact the submitting officer has reached a conclusion in that regard. Furthermore; these notes will be a major factor in developing a conceptualization of the SbC from the perspective of the officers submitting the original case file. Finally, the demographic information found in each of the cases determined to be suitable for this study will be collected and coded as a nominal measure.

The observational protocol for collecting the descriptive and reflective notes will be similar in style to the recording of field notes, but the concern of obtrusiveness is not an issue. As each case is reviewed notes will be recorded using a word processing program. A brief synopsis of the case will be followed by a detailed description of the incident as reported in the case file. The use of bulleted entries will assist in establishing the sequence of events as the incident developed into a deadly force encounter. This format will also allow for the recording of significant statements related to suicidal ideation or intent on the part of the actor, as well as other participants such as family, friends, witnesses, and police personnel. After each file has been thoroughly reviewed reflective notes will be recorded in a similar format. These notes will assist in classification of the file for consideration in including or excluding the file for final analysis. Notes on all files, inclusive or exclusive, will be maintained for use in this study.

The recording of demographic information for analysis of frequency distributions will be performed using the SPSS program. Variables will be measured as demographic or situational using a nominal scale. Demographic variables will focus on the suicidal actor and situational variables will record information relative to the incident, the threat and/or use of weapons and level of force used by the suicidal actor and police, a classification of the behavior of the suicidal actor as scripted or not, and the manner of death.

It is expected that demographic variables identifying gender, age, and race will be found in all of the cases examined. These variables will be coded numerically. Gender will be coded using the scheme 0=female, 1=male. Age will be rounded down to the nearest year and the coding scheme for race is 1=Asian, 2=Black, 3=Hispanic, 4=White, 5=Native American.

Other demographic variables will record the existence or absence of a criminal history as well as a history of substance abuse and/or mental illness. A psychiatric diagnosis will be coded as 0=no, 1=yes. Specific diagnosis will be recorded using the descriptive notes. Only medical diagnosis will be recorded. Speculative diagnosis by police, family or witnesses will be recorded using the descriptive notes. The use or threat of weapons by the suicidal actor will be recorded based on the identification of weapons in the preliminary review of the files. These include, but will not be limited to firearms, edged weapons, and blunt instruments such as a piece of pipe. In those cases where no weapon was used the descriptive notes will record the type of object that was used or perceived by the police as a weapon.

A portion of the variables will be dedicated to collecting pertinent information relative to the on-scene police personnel. The death or injury of police personnel will be coded as 0=no, 1=yes. The number, extent of injury, or the mechanism of death of police personnel will be recorded using the descriptive notes. The number of police personnel as well as supervisors will be recorded numerically. The level of force used by the police will be examined using a continuum consisting of five levels. Each level allows for a separate application of force and the continuum will ascend from the use of verbal commands, or constructive force, physical contact, physical force, mechanical force, to deadly force. The first level of force is constructive. The use of less lethal measures will be coded as 0=no, 1=yes, and the deployment of less lethal measures will be recorded in detail in the descriptive notes. The manner of death will be coded as 0=not determined/pending, 1=homicide, 2=suicide, 3=attempt. Scripted behavior will be coded as 0=no, 1=yes, and the determination of this coding will be based on the reflective notes of the principal

researcher.

CHAPTER 5

This study examined suicide-by-cop with the expectation that a conceptual model

describing how police practitioners view the phenomenon in a generalized sense could

be developed. The previous two chapters on research design and methodology

described how the data consisting of 61 individually conducted case studies were

selected, processed and analyzed for the purpose of this study.

A preliminary review of the data was conducted to determine what case studies would

be suitable for the present analysis, and to determine the scope and range of information

contained within the files. As a result of this initial analysis four cases studies were

excluded from the original N=61. Two of these files were case studies of SbC incidents

that had been previously examined by other NA attendees,[26] one file involved an

incident that was not related to civilian law enforcement, and one file was found to be

incomplete.[27] Overall, the final analysis resulted in a N=57. Twenty-six of these 57

cases (45%) were classified as being SbC based on the design criteria developed for

this study. The remaining 31 cases (54%) were determined not to be SbC for reasons

that will be discussed further in this chapter.

The discussion related to the analysis and findings of this research will begin with a

presentation of cases that were found to meet the definitional construct of SbC used in this

study. Additionally, this section will also present cases that contained sufficient

---

[26] These files were reviewed simultaneously due in large part to little to no variation in content. One file was
viewed as partially complete since the analysis was conducted as the case was still being investigated and
one case file was incomplete.

[27] It could not be determined if the file was incomplete when originally submitted, or if a substantial portion of
the file was lost or misfiled during collection or storage.

information to support the theory that the behavior of actors in SbC incidents can be described as scripted. Second, cases studies that were determined not to be SbC will be discussed with a focus on the dynamics of these cases that can account for a misclassification. Third, a conceptual model of how SbC is viewed by the officers who conducted the initial case studies will be constructed. Although this model will be limited in the ability to generalize it to a larger cohort, it will help to foster a better understanding of what SbC is, and more importantly, what it is not. Finally, demographic variables of the 26 SbC cases will be presented and discussed.

Confirming SbC Incidents

The decision to classify case studies examined in this research as SbC was based on the construct of a definition that narrowly focused on the intent and subsequent actions of the person engaged with police in a deadly force situation. Classification of a case as SbC required that evidence of suicidal intent involving a police use of deadly force vis-à-vis verbal or non-verbal communication could be identified, there is a possession, threat, attempt, or use of some form of lethal weapon by the suicidal actor involving a provocation of the police, and it could be shown that the actor voluntarily entered the drama.

In discussing those case studies that have been confirmed as SbC the cases will be grouped according to the type of incident that initially prompted a police response or action. The preliminary analysis of the initial N=61 revealed that reports of suicidal persons accounted for the largest grouping of cases by type of incident (n=9). The second highest grouping is incidents involving a reported crime, or an incident involving a self-initiated police investigation. Initially, case studies that involved the commission of a crime (n=6), specifically felonies, occurred less frequently than incidents involving domestic violence (n=8). However, in combining cases involving a report of a person armed with a firearm (n=7) the grouping for the crime category initially totaled 13. Table 6 illustrates that in the final analysis 10 cases (38.5%) involved the commission of a crime or a report of a person armed with a firearm. The third grouping includes cases that are of a nature that can be generally categorized as involving some form of domestic violence, which includes, but is not limited to, harassment, varying degrees of assault, destruction of property, threats and attempted murder. Preliminarily, eight cases of the initial N=61 were categorized as involving domestic violence. A closer examination of the data set included five additional cases of domestic violence raising the preliminary count to 13 (21%). Table 7 illustrates the final number of SbC cases involving some level of domestic violence between the suicidal actor, family members, or others involved in a relationship with the actor. There were a total of seven cases (26.9%) prompting a police response to an incident categorized as domestic violence. Further analysis of these seven cases reveals that in six cases (85.7%) alcohol and/or drugs were present in the system of the actor. In five cases (71.4%) alcohol was a factor, the use of drugs was noted in one case (14.2%), and drugs or alcohol was absent in one case (14.2%).

Table 6: Crime

0=no, 1=yes

		Frequency	Percent	Valid Percent	Cumulative Percent
Valid	0	16	61.5	61.5	61.5
	1	10	38.5	38.5	100.0
	Total	26	100.0	100.0	

Table 7: Domestic Violence

0=no, 1=yes

		Frequency	Percent	Valid Percent	Cumulative Percent
Valid	0	19	73.1	73.1	73.1
	1	7	26.9	26.9	100.0
	Total	26	100.0	100.0	

The final grouping will include any remaining SbC cases that were not categorized as suicidal, crime, or domestic violence. Cases will be discussed using a narrative format based on information from field notes. The identity of the suicidal actor will be discussed using artificial initials.

SbC and Crime

Man with a gun – Shots fired

This case involves CO, a partially disabled 47-year-old white male, whom family and friends describe as a recovering alcoholic who also suffers from depression. The disability prevents CO from maintaining steady employment and he sustains his income through benefits and menial work. CO had recently completed an alcohol detoxification program and was believed to be alcohol-free. The benefits that CO had been receiving had been recently stopped and friends described this as a significant life-event.

> It was just before midnight when the police were called reporting that a man had fired a gun in the vicinity of a local gas station. The first officer on the scene observes an adult male in the vicinity of the call and notices that a handgun is protruding from the man's front pants pocket. Without warning the man pulls the gun from his pocket and points it in the direction of the officer.

> Something caught the eye of the officer. The man's gun hand was shaking. Was this from nerves, the effects of alcohol, or something else? With the other hand the man was motioning to the officer as if to warn him to back away.

91

The officer orders the man to drop the weapon and then backs away from the immediate area using his police car. As additional police arrive and establish a perimeter the man enters a mobile camper that was parked behind the gas station.

While officers maintained their position the man was seen exiting the camper and he pointed the gun in the general direction of where officers were positioned behind cover. The officers yelled for the man to drop the gun. Dialogue was one-sided, the man, who did not comply with the officer's commands, kept the gun pointed at the officers, but he did not say anything at this point.

A police hostage negotiator arrives and enters the gas station next to the man's camper. A dialogue between the negotiator and the man begins and the negotiator learns CO's identity.

In talking with the negotiator CO discusses his desire to die and go to Heaven, and CO informs the negotiator that he wanted officers to shoot him in order to fulfill his desire.

The dialogue between the negotiator and CO alternated between CO's desire to have the police shoot him, and if that did not happen, CO threatened to commit suicide. Periodically CO used a flashlight to illuminate his head. When doing this CO would ask the negotiator if officers were able to see his head and if there was any particular way that he should turn his head.

One officer who was positioned near the camper during the standoff recalled CO stating that he did not want to hurt anybody, but would if he had to. This statement was preceded by, and followed with, statements regarding CO's intentions of having police shoot and kill him.

During the dialogue between the negotiator and CO the police allowed the owner of the gas station, who knew CO for over 15 years, to try and talk with him. At times CO used a cigarette lighter to illuminate his face and head creating a silhouette. The use of the lighter at this point would prove to be a significant departure from the ongoing dialogue between the negotiator and CO. CO was now threatening to start a fire in the camper if the officers did not shoot him. CO's actions resulted in a small fire within the camper. The negotiator wanted CO to extinguish the flames and at first he made an attempt to do so. For any number of reasons, CO was unsuccessful in putting the fire out and it quickly began to burn out of control forcing CO to flee the camper.

As CO exited the camper, armed with the handgun the negotiator left the safety of cover exposing him in an effort to maintain a dialogue with CO. CO began walking away from the camper with his gun hand extended toward officers in the immediate area. The negotiator tried to get CO to stop and he momentarily glanced over at the negotiator before continuing toward the officers.

CO closes the gap between the officers continuing to keep the gun leveled at the nearby officers. When he is less than 10 feet from the officers CO is shot.

The case study by the submitting officer contained a detailed synopsis and analysis of the case allowing for a thorough secondary analysis of CO's actions prior to and during this suicidal drama. The synopsis includes notations regarding the condition of the gun carried by CO and the fact that it was discovered to be empty. A search of the area after CO was shot revealed one live round in the vicinity of where he was standing when the first officer arrived. It was learned that CO owned the handgun, but it was not known for how long, or how proficient he was with the weapon. A check of the case study and police file did not uncover any reference to or any report related to the presence or absence of alcohol or drugs in CO's system. A cause of death was also not listed.

Without benefit of a formal definition of SbC the primary analysis of this case by the submitting officer focuses on CO's history of alcoholism, depression and a significant life-event that may well have been the catalyst for CO's actions. In the opinion of the submitting officer, CO's physical actions in illuminating his face and head, first with a flashlight and then with a cigarette lighter, where done with a belief and expectation that the result of these actions would be a bullet fired from police officer's weapon. The submitting officer supports this assertion by highlighting the conversation CO had with the negotiator when asking how he, CO, should turn his head. There were no indications in the synopsis, analysis, or the police reports that would suggest that CO was not coherent during the dialogue with the negotiator.

The actions of CO resulting in an initial police response may or may not have been intentional. CO may have been testing the weapon for functionality while contemplating

93

committing suicide. The single live round found in the area where CO was first observed may have been dropped intentionally or accidentally, and whether CO was aware of this or not is not known. When CO was observed pointing the gun at the first-responding officer the officer described CO's gun hand as shaking. With his free hand CO was seen waving at the officer as if to warn him to go away. Was this a man who was intent on committing suicide at that moment, or was SbC the option? The file contained statements from family and friends that gave insight into CO's troubles with his inability to work due to his disability, alcoholism, and depression. However, the file does not contain any information to suggest that CO had any history of suicidal ideation or attempts, or any indication that CO had planned the events on that fateful night. Regardless, with the arrival of the police SbC was now an option.

This case meets the definitional construct of SbC developed for this study. CO clearly communicated his desire to die, and in this case he specifically articulated expectations of police shooting him as the means to achieve this end. CO's actions when he exited the camper involved the use of a weapon resulting in the provocation of police.

The police in this case maintained a defensive posture that initially was not responsive to CO's demands that the police shoot and kill him. His actions when exiting the camper were contrary to police commands to drop the gun. By keeping the gun at the high-ready position while advancing on the police officers CO's actions were obviously threatening. CO's behavior in this sense is would meet the criteria of scripted behavior.

The Bank Robbery

This case is one of several in the original data set that had a limited synopsis and/or analysis completed by the submitting officer. The facts from this case, as with others, were determined by conducting a primary analysis of the file. The submission of a case such as this, and the absence of substantive information from the submitting officer, will be discussed further in this chapter.

TC, an ex-con, was a 28-year-old white male with a previous hospitalization for an attempted suicide. He robbed a local bank at 10:27 a.m. Police were notified of the bank robbery and a description of the subject and vehicle, a white limousine, was broadcast to local and state police. State troopers locate the vehicle on an Interstate highway, and after a brief motor vehicle chase TC is ordered from the limousine at gunpoint. During a brief standoff TC is yelling at the troopers that he was not going to return to jail. Ignoring the commands of the troopers TC moves suddenly and in such a way that it appears to the troopers that he is bringing something from behind his back. The troopers perceive this a threatening action and respond with deadly force. TC is wounded and survives.

> TC was in need of cash and devised a plan to rob a local bank. With no car available he contacts a limousine company and requests a pick-up from a motel that he had been staying at the past few days. TC instructed the driver to stop by the bank and to wait for him under the guise that he was conducting business in the bank.

> Once inside the bank TC passed a note to a teller demanding money. TC was not armed, nor was any mention of a weapon found in the investigative reports. With $900.00 in hand TC leaves the bank entering the limousine.

> TC told the driver that he was going to get some sleep and raised the dividing window. There was no other conversation between TC and the driver until the first police car pulled behind the limousine with the emergency lights on. TC asks the driver if he was speeding. A short time later the limousine driver pulls to the

95

shoulder of the road. Three state troopers are positioned behind the car and conduct a high-risk, or felony motor vehicle stop.

Using the PA system in the police car the troopers order the driver to turn the car off and remove the keys from the ignition. Their next command is for the driver to place the keys on the roof of the car. The driver is ordered to step form the car and raise his hands as high as he can. The troopers then order the driver to rotate in a complete circle keeping his hands in the air the entire time. After completing the circle the driver is ordered to walk backwards toward the troopers voices and is then taken into custody.

One trooper was moving with the driver toward one of the state police cars when the other troopers began the process for removing the remaining occupant in the car.

The same procedure will now be repeated with the passenger seated in the back of the limousine. TC is ordered from the car and the troopers determine that he matches the description of the man wanted for the bank robbery. TC exits the car with both of his hands in his jacket pockets. The troopers repeatedly order him to remove his hands from the jacket pockets. TC does not comply.

TC was standing at the rear of the limousine facing the troopers and was moving from side-to-side of the car. His hands at this point are underneath his jacket.

TC suddenly began yelling; "I'm not going to jail, your not taking me to jail, I won't go."

Without warning TC pulled his hands from inside his jacket in what is described by one of the troopers as a rapid movement. Bringing his hands together in front of him TC is now pointing in the direction of the troopers. Two of the troopers believe that TC is holding a black object in his hands.

One of the three troopers shot at TC and all three observed his jacket "puff up". The troopers were unsure if TC had in fact shot himself at this point.

The trooper with the driver of the limousine observed TC's actions and believed that TC was going to shoot pushed the driver to the ground.

TC did not fall and the troopers observed him place a hand back into the jacket. Again, TC pulled his hand out in a swift motion that was perceived by the troopers as threatening. TC moved toward the front of the limousine and fell to the ground.

The troopers advanced on TC and found him lying on the ground with both of his arms tucked underneath his body. TC refused repeated orders to bring his arms out from under his chest so that the troopers could check him for weapons.

96

TC was handcuffed and searched. No weapon was found. A wallet was found near where TC was standing when he was shot. The troopers each reported detecting a strong odor of an alcoholic beverage coming from TC.

TC stated, "I just want to die, why didn't you just kill me. I wanted you to shoot me."

TC was transported to a hospital were it was determined during treatment that his Blood Alcohol level was 0.14%. The choice not to drink and drive may have been the only smart decision that TC made that day.

At the hospital TC made several inculpatory statements as to why he acted and moved in the manner that he did. Described as alert and conscious TC engaged medical personnel in conversation. In talking with hospital staff TC made one statement, "I was trying to make them think I had a gun, I wanted to die, they'll feel bad that they had to shoot me, I tried to make them think I had a gun."

In speaking with one treating physician TC responded to the doctor's question as to why he did what he did with expletives and by stating that he wanted to die because he thought the officers would feel bad for having to shoot him. Within the context of the other statements made by TC this particular statement appears to be in the form of bravado than actual intent. Although it cannot be discounted that TC's intent may have been to use his death as a psychological ploy aimed at harming the officers.

TC was photographed in the hospital during treatment and in the photograph can be seen sticking out his tongue at the photographer in an act of defiance.

This case study did not contain a substantive synopsis or analysis of the file and was reviewed using a primary analysis of the data. The opinion of the submitting officer that this case raised to the level of SbC was obviously determined by the fact pattern in the case and the statements of TC, the troopers involved, as well the statements of attending medical personnel at the hospital.

TC's actions prior to and during the bank robbery offer no indication as to the completeness of any plan he had involving death or suicide as an option. The file did not reveal any evidence that TC was armed during the robbery, nor did he exhibit any behavior to suggest that he was prepared to confront police if stopped. Yet, when TC was ordered from the car he yelled to the troopers, informing them that he did not intend to return to jail. TC followed this statement with physical actions that were perceived by the troopers to be life threatening. Although TC did not possess a weapon, his quick mannerisms coupled with what appeared to be a dark colored object in his hands caused the troopers to respond to the actions with deadly force.

TC's motivation for his actions can be described as instrumental in nature. However, the fact that he did not have the instrumentality to carry out his assertion that he was not going to go back to jail he may have resorted to the next logical choice; to fake it. The issue can be raised that TC was attempting to take out his wallet and the troopers mistook this action as a threatening maneuver intended to produce a weapon, and had TC succumbed to his wounds this case would most likely not have been classified as SbC. The necessary requirement for communication of suicidal ideation was not evident until after TC was shot. Had he died at the scene his intent would not have been uncovered. However, the statements made by TC at the scene, in the hospital, and during subsequent interviews with F.B.I. agents that he wanted the troopers to shoot him supports the assertion that this was an attempt SbC. TC's actions were perceived by the troopers to be threatening and they reacted accordingly. The troopers were not interested in TC's identification. TC was expected to comply with the trooper's orders in a similar fashion to how the driver reacted. TC voluntarily asserted that he expected to be shot as a result of his actions and his behavior in this regard was scripted.

Shots Fired

This case begins as a self-initiated police response to shots fired in a large urban housing development. The synopsis of this case involves a detailed step-by-step description of the incident. The analysis, although less detailed than the synopsis, provides an insightful look into the recent history of the actor in this drama.

This drama unfolds in a rapidly developing series of events beginning with police officers responding to the sound of gunfire in a multi-story housing complex. As the officers enter the building they begin searching the area attempting to locate the origin of the shots. Making their way to the third floor they discover the lifeless body of an adult female victim. Small caliber shell casings are found on the floor near the victim's body. The search for the shooter is on.

Within minutes a police officer locates a Hispanic male on a sidewalk outside of the building where the shooting occurred. The male is armed with two weapons, a shotgun and handgun. A tense standoff begins when the actor points both weapons at his head. As quickly as it began, the drama ends when the actor lowers the shotgun at the officers and is shot.

The actor in this drama was identified as NY, a 44-year old Hispanic male with a history of problems. The case study documents a series of unstable relationships in NY's adult life that were impacted on by his violent behavior, often times involving weapons, chronic anger related issues, strong indicators of chronic alcoholism, and a previous suicide attempt.

> It was a mid-summer night and NY had been drinking; his blood alcohol level was found to be 0.17% at the time of his death that occurred shortly after he shot the victim.

> Something occurred between NY and the dead woman found by police on the third floor of the building putting NY on a path of self-destruction.

A police officer is walking a foot patrol when he hears gunshots coming from inside of the building. The officer enters the building moving in the general direction of where the shots were initially heard. A woman's body is found lying in a third floor hallway. Dressed in shorts and a blouse, the straps of her purse are looped over one arm. Spent shell casings are on the floor near the bloodied, lifeless body.

The police radio comes to life. A broadcast is given; "Shots fired." The search begins.

Outside of the building, on the sidewalk, a police officer encounters NY. In one hand NY is holding a handgun and in the other hand a shotgun. NY has both weapons pointed at his head.

The officer shouts at NY, "Drop the weapons. Drop the weapons." NY replies, "No."

Other police officers arrived. A chorus of commands to drop the weapons is met with a verbal response; "No." NY was also shaking his head side-to-side communicating a negative non-verbal response.

NY is holding the shotgun with the barrel pointed near his mouth. Suddenly, NY yells, "I can't do this." NY lowers the shotgun, leveling it at the police officers. Police officers react to NY's actions with deadly force.

The toxicological reports from the autopsy reveal that NY was intoxicated at the time of his death, and there were trace amounts of Cocaine in his system.

The analysis of this case as discussed in the initial case study focuses on the many facets of NY's personality and behavior. Although much of the analysis in the case study is speculative it helps to develop a portrait of NY that reveals a pattern of violent behavior involving weapons and threats, suicidal ideation with a failed attempted suicide, a history of unstable relationships, and the use and abuse of alcohol and other drugs.

What caused NY to kill at this time and place? What was he thinking at that moment? Was this a planned act of violence, or was it spontaneous, the pinnacle in an otherwise obvious cycle of violence? The answers to these questions are not found in the initial analysis. However, when closely examined through subsequent secondary analysis it is evident that

NY's behavior in this drama becomes compounded through a series of rapidly unfolding events resulting in his own death in what has been classified as SbC.

NY had a history of violent and aggressive behavior, yet he lacked the fortitude to kill himself. He could not complete his first suicide attempt when he contemplated jumping to his death from the roof of a multi-story building. Similarly, he was not capable of using a firearm to kill himself after he had just committed murder. NY's statement, "I can't do this." is key to the scripted nature of his actions. By lowering the weapon in the direction of the officer he was sure to be shot, and the likelihood that he would die as a result of his actions almost assured.

Evidence of Suicidal Behavior

Check the Welfare

This case was presented with a two-sentence synopsis of the incident describing the arrival of police officers in response to a request to check on the welfare of a man described by his sister as being suicidal. The synopsis provides a limited description of the events without benefit of any analysis of the case by the submitting officer. Based on secondary analysis of the preliminary police reports, statements, and follow-up investigative reports this case was classified as SbC.

The actor in this drama is DT, a 20-year old, white male, with a history of suicidal ideation and threats. In the days preceding his death DT had articulated to family members, his girlfriend, and others, that he intended to end his life. His threats were not taken lightly, prompting his sister to call police requesting assistance. Family members categorized DT as being crazy, but this appears to be more of a stereotypical response to his actions preceding his death. The file does not contain any evidence or documentation to support a

medical diagnosis of mental illness. DT's girlfriend revealed to police during an interview

after the incident that DT considered suicide as an option to stop the pain that he was

experiencing. The pain that DT felt was attributed to the ending of the relationship that he

had with the girlfriend in the past month. No cause or reason for the ending of the

relationship was found in the case file.

DT was in pain. His relationship with his girlfriend ended in the past month. The
future looked bleak for DT and he was not afraid to voice his thoughts regarding
suicide as a viable option to end that pain.

In the short span of time between the ending of the relationship and DT's death he
was described by family and friends as being depressed.

DT told his girlfriend that he was going to kill himself and that he would use a gun
in doing so. However, the girlfriend felt that the frequency of the threats without
direct action diminished the likelihood that DT would actually commit suicide.

Something or someone caused DT to reach the breaking point.

DT had been drinking during the evening. He had talked with his girlfriend and told
her that he was going to end the pain. She did not take him seriously at that time.

Initial threats to commit suicide involved the use of a gun. There were guns in his
home. DT called his mother and told her that he was intending to commit suicide
and that he was coming home to get a gun.

It was past midnight when DT first arrived at his mother's home prompting his
sister to call police and requesting their assistance in dealing with a suicidal DT.

Frantically, DT's family began hiding weapons. At this point DT was partially clad,
wearing only pants. The outside temperature was below freezing.

DT entered his mother's house in search of a gun. His brothers attempted to stop
him, but he is successful in getting a single-barrel shotgun.

DT leaves the area in his truck only to run off the road into a small stream.
Returning to the house he is discovered by a police officer sitting on his mother's
front porch. DT was holding a shotgun with the barrel of the gun in his mouth and

one foot was on the trigger. There was no trigger guard on this gun making it that much easier for DT to position his foot for the purpose of pulling the trigger.

The police officer begins screaming at DT to drop the gun. DT responds, "Fuck you I'm going to kill myself. I'm going to kill everybody." The officer describes DT as not being fazed by the presence of the police, nor the fact that weapons were pointed directly at him.

DT yells "Shoot me." "Kill me." The officer can hear DT's mother yelling, "Don't shoot him. That's what he wants."

During all of this DT removes the barrel from the shotgun from his mouth, pointing it at the officer and family members standing nearby.

In his final act DT lowers the shotgun and points it at the single police officer. The officer uses deadly force resulting in DT's death.

The shotgun, a single-barrel, was loaded.

Although the submitting officer did not analyze this case, the file contained sufficient information that allows for a categorization of SbC. The emotional state, behavior, and actions of DT leading up to his death reveal a thought process involving suicidal ideation. Earlier statements about suicide to his girlfriend were not taken seriously. DT may have made these earlier statements with an expectation of providing a necessary shock that could revive the relationship, but if that was his strategy it clearly was not working.

There was no evidence that DT considered SbC as an option. The arrival of the police was at the request of the family and there were no statements or communications from DT that would indicate that he expected that. DT's initial position, when discovered by the police officer, with the shotgun barrel in his mouth and his foot on the trigger is characteristic of how a person could commit suicide with that type of weapon. SbC was most likely not a considered option at that time. The changing dynamics of the incident, the proximity of DT's mother and her statement in response to DT yelling "Shoot me" may well have been a catalyst for DT's final action of pointing the shotgun at the officer. Yet the initial case study does not examine any of these facts presenting the case only on face value. The absence of a substantive analysis of the incident, presenting the case on face value, supports the legitimate criticism of how SbC is presently defined and classified.

Life can be cruel

The synopsis and subsequent analysis of this case provide strong evidence of pre-planning and provocation on the part of a suicidal person intent on committing suicide, specifically SbC. The submitting officer gives a detailed analysis of the actions of the suicidal actor, focusing on the actions intended to provoke police officers into resorting to deadly force. This analysis describes in detail what has been operationalized for the purpose of this study as scripted behavior. This case helps to show the cause and effect of scripted behavior in SbC.

CC was a 45-year old, white male, who had recently experienced what can best be categorized as tragic major life events. Involved in a common-law relationship with a woman for 25 years CC adopted his wife's son. CC had suffered a serious job-related injury two-years prior to the incident that caused him significant pain and suffering. Compounding his physical pain CC's adoptive son had recently died as a result of a disease. CC's dog, which he also cherished, died about the same time. A month prior to the incident CC and his wife were forced to move from their home that was due to be demolished. Just four days before the incident CC's wife was killed in an auto-pedestrian accident, and a day after that accident his wife's dog died from an illness. Life for CC had become unbearable, and according to his mother CC "just exploded."

CC had moved into his mother's trailer home the previous month where he was living when his life tragically and rapidly disintegrates. CC was taking Valium since the death of his wife and is believed to be drinking as the incident unfolds.

CC's mother was aware of CC taking at least seven Valium in the hours leading up to the incident. At one point CC's mother witnessed him point the shotgun at his neck. They talked about suicide and CC's mother tried to explain to him that his wife would not want him to die as he was describing it.

CC's mother called a friend and recounted what CC was considering and had done up to that point. CC's mother was advised to leave the trailer and the friend contacted police.

Local police were alerted to a report of a man at a local trailer park with a gun pointed to his head. As police arrive they begin to evacuate people in nearby trailer homes. Residents report that CC has fired a shotgun into the air three times.

When the police first arrive they meet with CC's mother who briefs them on his condition and state of mind. CC was a man known for his temper. During arguments with his mother he would be quick to shout, "Go ahead call the cops."

Since the mother initially left the trailer it was unknown what CC was doing. The police let her go back into the trailer to check on CC at that time. CC is sleeping in a chair. He is holding the shotgun and the hammer on the gun is cocked. She contemplates removing the weapon from his hands, but CC begins moving. At this point she leaves the trailer.

Shortly after CC exits the trailer and states, "I'll shoot." CC's mother believed at that moment that CC wanted to die, but did not have the nerve to complete the act on his own. The thought that CC was going to attempt to have the police kill him was becoming a strong possibility.

The initial attempts to make contact with CC reveal that he is despondent and is requesting the police to kill him. A police sergeant spoke with CC who informed the officer that he had nothing to live for. He told the sergeant that he lost his family and that he was not going to go to jail. CC told the sergeant that he wanted to die and stated, "If you come inside I will issue fire."

During this CC indicated to the sergeant that he, CC, was familiar with how police operate and that if he came out shooting the police would kill him.

As dialogue continues CC exists the trailer and fires the shotgun at a police officer that is positioned behind a police vehicle. The police officers do not return fire at this time.

The sergeant tried to convince CC that there was help for him. CC hung up. Dialogue ends when CC disables the telephone and the officers on the scene request a police tactical unit.

The sergeant who originally spoke with CC was the initial negotiator and this officer continued to make attempts to contact CC. An hour into the incident the sergeant was able to make contact with CC. CC told the officer that he was coming out of the trailer in five minutes and said, "It's time." CC then hung up. CC exited the trailer and fired the shotgun into the air. Police did not return fire. CC walked around in front of the trailer for a brief period of time and then went back in.

Phone contact was re-established at that point. CC answered the phone and asked the officer why police did not shoot him. The officer responded that they were there to help. Five minutes later CC again exited the trailer and fired twice at officers behind cover. Officers did not return fire.

At this point a senior hostage negotiator who had been monitoring and assessing the incident during the earlier negotiations with CC assumed control.

CC told the senior negotiator that he wanted to die "today" and that he wanted the cops to do it. The negotiator spoke to CC about making the cops kill him and what that would do to them, meaning the officers involved. CC did not care about how his actions impacted on those officers he just wanted to die.

Why the cops? What brought CC to this point? A critical piece of information in this regard emerged. CC blamed the system, including the police, for not charging the driver in the accident that killed his wife. This would prove to be a pivotal point. The phone line went dead. CC had cut the line.

The police were preparing to re-establish communications with CC through the use of a specially equipped vehicle. Suddenly CC exited the trailer with the shotgun. He turned toward officers lowering the shotgun in their direction. He had fired twice at police already. Officers opened fire. CC died from his wounds.

The crime scene report notes that the shotgun CC was holding when he was shot and killed was loaded.

The analysis of this case is one of the few found in the data set that examines the totality of the incident with a strong emphasis on the minutia of CC's actions. The initial case study explores the significant life stressors that occurred in CC's life before the incident allowing for an understanding of his state of mind without making a justification for his actions.

A critical piece of information found in this particular case study was a transcript of the radio and hostage negotiation logs. These transcripts reveal valuable information into CC's state of mind and the police reactions to his demands and actions. Although this study is not focused on the actions of police during these incidents this case evidenced a great deal of restraint by on-scene police personnel. Furthermore, these transcripts help to portray an accurate picture of how scripted behavior on the part of the suicidal actor will play out. CC's actions in firing the shotgun at police on more than one occasion and his final actions of lowering the shotgun at police before being shot were in anticipation and expectation of a deadly force response by police officers.

Notwithstanding the wealth of information found in the file, and the superior case study that was conducted, there is one vital piece of information that was not found in any of the reports or documents. There was no autopsy report or mention of any toxicological report on the presence and/or levels of drugs or alcohol in CC's body at the time of his death. Police reports contained in the file reference the fact that CC's speech was slurred at times and this may have been caused by the use of the Valium, which was not prescribed to CC and he obtained it illegally according to his mother. Just how much of the sedative did CC take, and to what level would he be considered incapable of being cognitive of what his actions would cause are not known.

A Cry for Help

This case study contained an extensive synopsis of the incident with a minimal analysis of past behavior involving suicidal ideation, threats, and other types of risky behavior. The submitting officer relied on a review of the relevant literature in classifying this case as victim-precipitated homicide.

PP was a 48-year old, white male, who was described by family members as an alcoholic who would become mean and irrational when drinking. PP was diagnosed with Posttraumatic Stress Disorder and Obsessive-Compulsive Disorder, both of which are listed as Anxiety Disorders in the DSM-IV. The incident unfolded three days before PP's 49th birthday, a fact that was not mentioned in any of the reports or statements.

PP's past history involved several threats to commit suicide and one instance involving a standoff with police. During that incident PP was armed with a small caliber handgun. The incident was resolved when police convinced PP to drop the weapon, which he did, and he was then taken into custody. This incident is significant in that PP has a point of reference of how police deal with an armed suicidal person. Although not directly mentioned in the case study, or in the investigation of the present case, the past incident becomes a knowledge base for PP in any future dealings he may have with the police.

> It is three days before his 49th birthday. According to his wife, PP has been acting irrational and was depressed.
>
> PP had spoken with his son and the son's girlfriend earlier in the day and had told them that he was going to "fight the police and kill some cops." This statement reveals something about PP's train of thought and the possibility that a suicidal plan involving SbC was formulating.
>
> The girlfriend had called the son later that day as the incident was unfolding. PP answered the phone and spoke again with the girlfriend. She described PP as being distraught and his conversation at times focused on his disdain for government and how they can ruin your life. PP was bitter after winning a substantial sum in a lottery only to have his winnings and home taxed at what he felt was an exorbitant rate. He also told the girl that he had shot some rounds off and that the police were on their way and that he was going to fight them when they arrived. PP's final request was for the girl to come over and talk with him. She agreed and told him that she would be there in 20 minutes.

PP told the girl he loved her like a daughter and that everything would be fine. However, his demeanor quickly changed when he informed her that if she were not there in 20 minutes he would shoot himself.

Within five minutes of that call the girlfriend learned that PP had taken his son hostage.

It is late afternoon and a loud bang and breaking glass is heard coming from the rear of their home and PP's wife sends her son to investigate.

PP's son enters a shed in the rear of the home and finds his father and notices that there was a hole in the roof of the shed.

PP's son yells at his father. He asks him, "Are you crazy?" He then tells his father that someone may call the police and that he, PP, could go to jail. The son tries unsuccessfully in talking his father into putting down the gun.

PP responds to his son by telling him that he does not intend to hurt him and requests him to come into the shed with him, but he refused.

The son had returned to the house when he heard a second shot ring out. He returned to the shed to find his father sitting with the shotgun in his mouth.

PP's wife leaves the home and drives to the local police department to report the incident. She informs the police that PP has tried to commit suicide in the past and that she was surprised to learn that he had a shotgun. As far as she could remember PP had a shotgun in the past, but the gun had been pawned at a local shop.

PP returned to the house. Finding his son inside he informs the son, "You're my hostage." The son pleads with PP to let him go, but he refuses. PP did tell his son that he would not hurt him and that he did not want him to leave. For whatever reason the son did not leave. It could not be determined from the case file if this action was voluntary or compelled.

Police arrived at PP's home and tried several times to establish telephone contact with him. What they did not know at this time was that PP's son was still present and in fact PP had taken him hostage. The son would later tell police officers that he felt his father wanted the police to kill him because he "did not have the balls to shoot himself."

The police used a public address system in an attempt to make contact with PP.

Officers observed PP leave the house and enter the shed located in the rear of the home. An officer made contact with PP. PP shouted at the officer that he wanted to die. PP wanted the police to shoot him.

The officer pleaded with PP to come out of the shed, but he refused. Instead PP requested the officer to come into the shed where he was. This was a repetitive request by PP. The initial request was of his son when he first came out to the shed when PP fired the first round.

The officer continued to converse with PP. They talked about the medications that PP was taking. Again, PP requested the officer to shoot him.

During the course of this standoff PP would leave the shed and re-enter the home. Officers within the inner perimeter observed PP carrying a shotgun at various times during these back-and-forth trips.

PP was becoming increasingly agitated threatening to shoot at officers if they did not shoot him.

PP exited the home and officers requested that he put the gun down. Surprisingly he did. The shotgun was leaning against a fence within arms reach of PP.

A SWAT team began advancing on PP ordering him to drop to the ground. PP was startled by these actions and turned back toward the gun. After grabbing the shotgun PP turned back toward the advancing officers and began to raise the gun at them.

The officer who initially established dialogue with PP, who was positioned off to the side of the advancing SWAT team, fired several rounds at PP. PP turned toward that officer who fired additional rounds at him.

PP was transported to an area hospital where he died from his wounds. The toxicology report reveals that PP's Blood Alcohol Content was 0.22% at the time of his death.

A search of the area in the shed where PP had been going repeatedly during the incident revealed a half-consumed bottle of whiskey.

The initial case study analysis highlighted sufficient relevant information to support a classification of SbC. However, the file and subsequent analysis are mute on factors related to PP's alcoholism. A 0.22% BAC involves a significant level of alcohol consumption. What would help to clarify what was PP's state-of-mind would be information regarding any pattern in his drinking behavior. Was he a daily or maintenance drinker? Was he a binge drinker? How much did he normally consume at any given time, and was this behavior acceptable within his social circle?

Although it may be argued that PP was too intoxicated to be cognizant of what cause and effect his actions would have it is evident based on his statements to family members and police present at the scene PP expected to die that afternoon. That expectation was being scripted by PP into an SbC incident.

Domestic Violence

The cases that will be discussed in this section have been classified or categorized as domestic violence either by the originating investigating law enforcement agency or by the officer conducting the initial case study.

Decide What You Want

The submitting officer provides a detailed synopsis of the events leading up to and resulting in SbC by a person with a history of suicidal ideation and a previous suicide attempt. The analysis of this case focuses on the statements of the suicidal actor as a primary indicator of intent to commit SbC.

The case involves LC a 45-year old, white male, who was described by family members as being an alcoholic. LC's adult life was full of periods of suicidal ideation including one attempt involving the slashing if his wrists and another incident where his brother talked him out of committing suicide. A military veteran, LC was recommended for psychiatric assistance upon separation from service, but according to family members he did not follow through. All accounts of LC's adult life include issues related to alcoholism and suicidal ideation, but there is no reference or mention as to what a precipitating cause may

have been.

The incident begins with LC's wife calling police to report an incidence of domestic violence. Although there is no evidence of an overt act of violence being committed by LC at this time the situation has all the potential.

LC is intoxicated and has made a comment to his wife that worried her. They exchange words about the comment to which LC replies, "You better decide what you want." The exact nature of that comment was not revealed, but it was enough for her to call police. As could be expected, LC's drinking was a source of marital problems.

LC's wife told the police dispatcher that LC owned several shotguns and that she was concerned for his well-being. The dispatcher instructed the wife to leave the residence. As she did so she recalled the sound of a shotgun action be worked a number of times.

LC was an avid hunter and very familiar with the workings of a shotgun. His wife informed officers that he often would keep a shotgun underneath his bed.

When police arrived the wife informed them that when she left the home several lights were on. The home was now in complete darkness.

Officers approached the home and announced their presence. LC allowed the officers to enter the home. No weapons were visible.

The officers informed LC that they were there to check on his well-being. LC volunteered that he had been "messing around" with some shotguns."

LC then stated, "The only way to get away from all of this mess is to just end it all."

The officers spoke with LC about the availability of social services that could help in this type of situation. LC responded, "The only way you can help me is to just shoot me. Just kill me and that will solve everything."

The officers continued to talk with LC with the hope of convincing him to agree to a self-committal to a mental health facility. LC was not interested. He began talking about his experiences in Vietnam. This caused LC to become emotional and he told the officers how he just wanted to stop putting his wife and daughter through so much trouble.

LC would tell the officers that if they really cared about helping him then they would "Take your guns out and just shoot me."

The officers realized that LC was not going to agree to a voluntary commitment and attempts were being made to request the wife to consider an involuntary commitment.

The dialogue with LC continued and at times he would begin to cry. One officer suggested that LC consider the local Veterans Administration for help. LC expressed a strong dissatisfaction with this option.

At one point LC told the officers that he considered committing suicide by driving his car at a high rate of speed into a fixed object. Without the benefit of formulating a response the police officers were surprised to see LC bolt from the chair that he was sitting in at the time and run from the room. One officer tried to stop him but could not.

LC ran through the darkened house into a room.

The officers followed illuminating the hallway with their flashlights. An officer shown the light into a room that LC ran into. LC was retrieving a shotgun from underneath the bed.

The officers retreated into the hallway and sought cover.

LC exited the room with the shotgun at waist level.

The officers yelled at LC to drop the gun. He replied, "No way."

LC raised the shotgun to his shoulder and pointed the gun at one of the officers. The officers opened fire. LC was struck numerous times.

The shotgun LC was holding when he pointed it at the officer was unloaded and had not been not fired.

The toxicological report from the autopsy reveals that LC's Blood Alcohol Content at the time of his death was 0.208%.

The case study identifies LC's statements as being the most insightful element in trying to determine what his intent was. Throughout this drama LC requested the police officers to shoot and kill him. These statements were made while LC was sitting on a couch in the living room of his own home. The incident was spread out over a period of 1 hour and 20 minutes. During this period LC was not drinking and the affects of any earlier drinking were diminishing.

113

As with a previously discussed case the true nature of LC's alcoholism is not known. To what extent did or could he function while intoxicated? LC's history as an alcoholic would help provide valuable information as to his abilities as a result of drinking.

His wife had reported to police that LC often would keep a shotgun underneath his bed. When LC bolted from the living room he ran into a bedroom and retrieved a shotgun from underneath a bed. This was obviously something that LC was aware of and was capable of responding to with a level of agility that exceeded that of the officers who were dealing with him in a face-to-face manner. Whether or not LC was aware of the shotgun being loaded or unloaded due to his level of intoxication is debatable. This was not a fall-down drunkard. LC was contemplating something while he was sitting there and he was revealing this to the officers who were present with repeated requests for the officers to shoot him.

The tipping point in this drama was when LC mentioned a prior notion that he had about committing suicide by driving at a high rate of speed into a fixed object. Did LC come to the realization that he was not capable of killing himself? Would LC have to use a proxy to complete the necessary violent act? Was SbC the solution to LC's problems? Based on the totality of the circumstances involving LC's fixation on SbC and his final actions in retrieving the shotgun the single answer to each of these questions would be an affirmative one.

Mother – Son Dispute
An excellent synopsis and detailed analysis in the case study allows for a comprehensive secondary analysis of a case involving a young man experiencing emotional and mental problems as the result of a head injury. Without extensive probing into all of the facts

surrounding the actions prior to and during the incident as well as statements made by the

actor in this drama this case could easily have been excluded from consideration based

solely on the medical and mental status of the actor. However, there is sufficient evidence

to support the assertion that the actor was aware of the ramifications of his actions, and that

the actions could and would result in his death.

MO was 28-year old, black male, who suffered a severe brain injury as the result of an

assault that occurred the previous year. MO was clinically diagnosed with Major

Depression (Axis I) as a result of the brain injury. Additionally, MO was diagnosed with

Severe Multiple Stressors (Axis IV) and was prescribed medication to assist him in coping.

MO had been hospitalized as a juvenile due to behavioral problems and his mother was

reported to have suffered from depression. The incident begins with an argument between

MO and his mother that rose to a level of a domestic violence ultimately ending with MO's

death as a result of SbC.

> Things are going bad between MO and his mother. They are arguing and things
> between them are extremely tense.
>
> The day after the argument MO's mother offers to bring MO to a bus depot and buy
> him a one-way ticket to anywhere he wants to go. This infuriates MO and they
> continue to argue. MO's mother attempts to dial 9-1-1 and request police assistance
> in removing MO from the house. MO knocks the phone from his mother's hand, an
> action that results in a struggle between MO and his mother's boyfriend.
>
> The police are finally notified. The report is that MO has gone "crazy" and that he
> is armed with a knife. The caller alerts police to the fact that MO is attempting to
> kill himself with the knife, and that he is making statements indicating that he wants
> the police to kill him.
>
> At one point before the police arrive MO lifts his shirt and threatens to kill himself
> in the presence of his mother. Admittedly, the mother looks at MO in such a way
> that her affect communicates a feeling of indifference to his threats. The reaction of

115

MO's mother to his threat has a profound impact on him and his articulation of suicidal ideation increases dramatically at this point.

MO states, "The police are gonna kill me tonight." His mother replies, "You don't want that to happen." MO responds, "I'm gonna make 'em kill me tonight."

MO's mother continues to try and reason with him. His only reply was "No, they're gonna kill me tonight."

The police arrive at this point and MO charges at the approaching officers with the knife in his hand.

The officers retreat as they request MO to put the knife down. The officers were trying to put time and distance between them and MO. MO's mother acknowledged that the officers were making every effort to keep MO from advancing toward them.

MO yells, "If she doesn't want me, you're going to have to kill me." As he was stating this MO was raising the knife over his head and continuing to close the distance between him and the officers.

The officers are now yelling for MO to drop the weapon. He is yelling back, "Shoot me! Shoot me!"

By this time the officers had retreated back over two hundred feet. MO continued to advance with the knife raised above his shoulder.

MO's advancement on the officers reached the breaking point. Shots were fired at MO as he continued to advance. MO died as a result of his injuries.

As a result of the traumatic brain injury suffered by MO his mental and emotional illness present significant challenges when considering his cognitive ability to understand and appreciate his actions. There are clear indications in the original file that demonstrate MO's behavior changes considerably when he is not taking prescribed medications. There is no mention in the reports, statements or other documents to suggest that MO was or was not taking his medications when he began arguing with his mother the day before his death. Yet, MO's statements regarding his desire to die, specifically by having the police shoot

116

him, coupled with his threatening actions toward officers are clear enough to suggest his understanding of the these statements along with the likely consequences of his actions.

That night MO had certain expectations. He threatened to commit suicide and his mother expressed indifference to these threats. MO was angry. What started all of this was his mother's attempt to give him a virtual one-way ticket to anywhere. If his mother did not want him, MO reasoned, there was no point in living. When he threatened to kill himself insult was added to injury. His mother communicated the message to him that she did not care if he did kill himself. What could be worse? MO's actions toward the police officers were expected to cause a certain response, but that also failed to meet his expectations. MO's continued advancement toward the officers can be described as scripted. MO pushed the envelope until the officers were forced in the proverbial corner and finally reacted with deadly force.

Excluded Cases

As with any research there will be cases that will be excluded from analysis for any number of reasons. For the purpose of this research cases were excluded for three primary reasons; incompleteness of the file, not meeting the definitional criteria of SbC that was operationalized for this study, or evidence within the file that the actor was not coherent or was suffering from severe mental illness. At the onset of data analysis for this study the N=61 included all of the case studies that had been classified as SbC by police officers as a part of an educational program at the FBI National Academy. Numerically the final data set in this study was far less robust and accounted for 42.6 % (n=26) of the initial data set

(N=61). The significance of the variance in percentages from the initial to the final analysis will be discussed in the conclusion of this report.

Unknown Intentions

This case is presented with a wealth of material including audiotapes, slides, and photographs of the scene none of which helps to support or justify classifying the case as SbC. The submitting officer provides a one-page synopsis that does not examine or consider the history or state of mind of the actor.

KK was a 32-year old, white male with a history of mental illness. A previous suicide attempt left him severely disfigured. The incident begins with KK notifying local police that he had stabbed his mother. Local and state police officers are dispatched and KK is fatally wounded after he advanced on the officers with a length of pipe held over his head in a menacing manner.

> Police receive a 9-1-1 call reporting a stabbing. The caller informed the operator that he was responsible for stabbing and killing the female victim.
>
> Available officers are dispatched to the reported location where KK lived with his mother. Three local officers and one state trooper were assigned. The local officers were familiar with KK and his history of problems involving his mental illness.
>
> When the officers arrived at KK's home they discovered his mother's lifeless body in an upstairs bedroom. A bloodied knife was found in the living room.
>
> A search of the home did not locate KK or anyone else. The officers began to search the property and quickly discovered a shotgun in a car parked near the house.
>
> The lights in a nearby building attracted the attention of the officers. As they approached the building the officers encountered KK standing near a piece of farm equipment. A local officer recognized KK who was seen holding a metal object in his hands.

The trooper was inside of the home when the officers located KK and responded to their verbal commands ordering KK to drop a weapon. As the trooper approached KK's position he noticed the object that KK was holding. The trooper described the object as a piece of pipe approximately 18-24 inches in length. KK was swinging the pipe back and forth alongside his leg at that point.

The officers could not immediately discern what the object was. It had the appearance of a barrel of a shotgun. KK was ordered to drop the weapon. The commands were repeated several times. KK began to advance toward the officers who attempted to maintain a safe distance by backing away.

KK began to run at the officers rapidly closing the distance. The trooper yelled at KK to drop the weapon. This caused KK to turn toward the trooper continuing his charge.

With the gap between KK and the officers closing it became clear that the object KK was holding was a long piece of metal pipe. As he advanced on the officers turning toward the trooper KK raised the pipe over his head. A vehicle blocked the trooper's retreat. With KK literally on top of him the trooper fired at KK stepping aside as his body fell to the ground.

The submission of this case is not supported with any type of analysis or facts that can justify or legitimize classifying the case as indicative of SbC. As with many cases that fall within this category the actions of the actor in light of the circumstances are viewed as suicidal, hence the classification. This approach tends to view actions as axiomatic of intent, and it is this type of subjective determination, not supported by fact that is a primary justification in questioning how cases are presently classified SbC.

Was KK suicidal? Possibly. The night before this incident he had been involved in a minor motor vehicle accident. One of the on-scene officers, who was present when KK was shot, observed lacerations on KK's neck while investigating that accident. The officer categorized these wounds as appearing to be self-inflicted. Was he testing a desire to commit suicide? Again, possible, but the file is void of any evidence or facts the suggest KK was contemplating or moving in this direction.

119

Was KK's death SbC? Not likely. KK was armed with a weapon and he did enter the deadly force drama when he advanced on the police officers raising the pipe, but the required communication of suicidal intent was clearly absent both before and during the incident. Aside from this case not meeting the definitional criteria of SbC a second consideration focuses on KK's motive and intent. Without sufficient information in the case file or the initial case study to support further analysis an objective determination is not possible.

Interrupted by a bullet

The following case has all of the indicators that could allow for a classification of SbC including a similar past incident that was resolved without the use of deadly force. However, a bullet from a police sniper interrupts the final actions of the actor in the present case. The submitting officer focuses more on police tactics and the goals of the media in covering police incidents live and on-camera as a result of this incident than on the issue of SbC.

The case involves BC a 25-year old, white female, with a history of suicidal ideation and two attempts. BC's actions in this case can objectively be described as intended to attract the attention of police. What is subject to debate is BC's ultimate intentions and were they accelerated vis-à-vis police tactics?

BC was upset. She was experiencing a problem in her relationship with her husband. This was compounded by financial difficulties. Approximately 5 months before her death BC had attempted to commit suicide by swallowing pills. This attempt was unsuccessful. Whatever BC ingested her body rejected. Her attempt ended when she vomited.

BC was still intent on committing suicide at that moment. She took a handgun from another area of the home and returned to the bathroom where she had vomited after her first attempt.

Locking herself in the bathroom she contacted her husband and told him of her plans to kill herself. She told her husband that she was in the shower to prevent making a mess.

BC's husband called the police.

When police arrived they forced entry into the bathroom. BC was nude, standing in the shower with the showerhead in one hand. BC's other hand was hidden between her legs and the officers could not detect what she was holding.

One officer attempted to cover BC's naked body requesting her to come out of the shower.

BC yelled, "Fuck you, I'll show you something." BC suddenly raised the hand that she had hidden between her legs and pointed a .45 caliber semi-automatic pistol at the officers.

When BC first revealed the gun the slide was locked to the rear. As she raised the gun in the direction of the officers BC released the slide on the gun. This action left the hammer on the gun cocked.

At one point BC pointed the gun at her head. She told the officers that she did not intend to shoot them.

BC reportedly knew the gun was unloaded and she had relayed to someone after the incident that the gun was merely to keep the officers away from her.

The officers took cover and requested assistance. A SWAT team and hostage negotiator was dispatched.

BC requested that either the officers leave or shoot her so she would not have to shoot herself.

Ultimately, BC surrendered to the police.

The criminal charges in that incident were later dropper after BC was referred for psychiatric evaluation.

BC left a note in this instance.

Nothing else remarkable about BC was reported, or found within the file.

The day of the next incident BC passed a police car that was traveling at 70-mph. Her speed was clocked at 90-mph.

BC's actions prompted a protracted police-pursuit over several miles of rural highways.

Finally, and without warning, BC pulled the minivan that she was driving to the side of the road.

Officers used the public address system from one of the police cars in an attempt to communicate with BC. BC did not reply or indicate acknowledgement of the officers.

Officers approached her vehicle and quickly noticed that she was holding a gun with both hands. The officers retreated from alongside the vehicle. As they retreated the officers ordered BC to place the gun on the dashboard. BC responded by giving the officers the finger and pointing the gun out of the van's window.

An officer with a rifle establishes a position for a shot if necessary. The officer is authorized to use deadly force if BC presents a threat.

Orders for BC to exit the minivan are ignored.

BC's only replies to police commands at this point are terse replies of "No."

Believing that BC does not speak or understand English an officer attempts to converse with her in Spanish. BC replies that she speaks English.

As SWAT arrives BC exits the minivan. The arrival of SWAT and BC's exit from the vehicle are likely coincidental and are not believed to be connected.

BC walks around to the front of the van. One officer relates that BC is holding the gun at waist level at this point. Another officer believes that the hammer of the weapon is cocked.

What happens next is a matter of contention. The distance between BC and on-scene officers is considered a sufficient buffer under the circumstances. The hand that BC is holding the weapon begins to move. Before the hand is raised to an appreciable height the officer who pre-positioned with the rifle fires a single shot killing BC.

By way of past behavior BC had demonstrated a desire to die. She also demonstrated a level of familiarity with firearms, specifically handguns. Her behavior in the present case was clearly risky and likely to cause her death as it did. However, the scale fails to tip in the direction that allows for a definitive categorization of her final actions, by beginning to raise her arm, as an offensive or suicidal act.

During the course of this incident BC was within speaking distance of police officers. The communication between BC and the police was curt and to the point. She was not adhering to their commands, but she was not making any demands of her own. What were her intentions? Was she prepared to surrender the weapon as she did in the previous incident? Was she going to commit suicide? The answer to either question could be an affirmative one.

As with the previous case this case presents operational issues that fail to meet definitional criteria. True, BC was armed. The question of whether or not she voluntarily entered the final act of this script is debatable and therefore problematic. The absence of any type or form of communication from BC as to her intent of suicide or any other action is without question absent. Here again lies the problem of subjectively viewing an action(s) as axiomatic of intent.

A similar case also ends with a bullet fired from the rifle of a police sniper. This case involves BC (no relation to the previous case) an 18-year old, white male who was killed while looking out of a window during a hostage situation.

123

The case synopsis is two pages in length and only provides details about the incident, a

protracted hostage incident occurring after the actor killed three college roommates. The

incident ended with a sniper's bullet killing BC. There is no analysis of the incident and it

is extremely difficult to consider this SbC based solely on the synopsis. Based on

interviews found in the case file there are references to statements attributed to BC that

point toward a consideration of SbC. However, as in the previous case BC's actions and/or

intentions are stopped as a result of a police action.[28]

> The incident involves a young man who shoots and kills three of his roommates in
> the home they shared. After this triple-homicide BC steals a vehicle and drives to
> another college town arriving several hours later. BC travels to this college to seek
> out a former girlfriend. He makes attempts to find her and learns that she will return
> to her dorm room around 9:30 a.m.

> The girl returns and as she enters her room she is followed by BC. She asks him to
> leave and he shows her a gun and tells her that he has killed his roommates. Upon
> learning that the police were on the way he became angry with the girlfriend and
> shot her in the foot with a handgun. By this time BC has a total of three hostages.

> SWAT was called and hostage negotiations began. BC agrees to release a hostage
> in exchange for soda. The negotiator reports that BC is very erratic in his behavior.
> BC was making outlandish demands for morphine and cigarettes. He appears at the
> dorm window and is shot by a sniper.

> The synopsis gives no clue as to why this case is classified as SbC. A hand written
> note initially started by one of the hostages at the direction of BC is addressed to
> BC's father. It is not clear that this was a suicide note, or an apology for the triple-
> homicide. BC does give away property to a friend in the letter and leaves $185.00
> in cash in the envelope. BC does make reference to it being all over during the
> hostage incident, but the drama ends after it is believed that the possibility of BC
> killing the hostages is highly probable. A sniper-initiated assault results in BC being
> shot while leaning out of a 4th floor window. SWAT breaches the dorm room door
> and find BC one the ground due to a rifle shot to the throat.

> In an otherwise voluminous file, there is only one reference to any type of
> communication by BC that could relate to SbC or suicide. BC states at one point,

---

[28] The fact that this case is not classified as a SbC in no way infers any doubt as to the course of action of the
    police personnel on the scene. The tactical operation that was put into place was clearly conducted as a life-
    saving mechanism intended to prevent any harm to the hostages.

"They'll have to kill me." This statement was reportedly made by BC during the hostage incident. It is paraphrased that BC stated he would rather die than go to jail.

Another hostage victim is reported to have heard BC state that if he has to he will begin shooting in the air or outside so that police will kill him. According to this victim BC had placed the gun between his eyes 3-4 times during the incident. All of this occurs before BC shoots the former girlfriend in the foot. Another hostage reports that BC stated the only way he was leaving was in a body bag.

A news article reports that the former girlfriend was aware that BC was looking out of the dorm room window and he most likely knew there were snipers posted. His actions before the shooting may well have been the proximate cause for his death, but it is not clear of his actions were intended to cause his death. Photographs of the incident seconds before the shooting shows one of the female hostages looking out of the window followed a short time later by BC.

A handwritten statement from one of the female hostages mentions BC's awareness of the police, but he questions who called the police.

The medical examiners report indicates the presence of ephedrine in BC's system. One hostage notes that BC informed the hostages at one point that he has not slept or eaten in days.

The final analysis of this case stops with the death of BC as the result of being shot by the police sniper. What assisted in reaching the conclusion that this was not SbC was an extensive collection of real-time photographs of the incident as it unfolded. One critical photograph was taken just before BC was shot. This photograph shows BC looking from the 4th floor room where he was holding the hostages. The photograph is best described as revealing a person who is surveying the scene. The fact that this instance presented itself as the best opportunity to neutralize the threat that BC posed to the hostages was fortuitous for the police, not BC.

Was BC on the path of committing suicide, specifically SbC? Possibly, but the fact that his actions were preempted by police action eliminates a necessary definitional criteria needed to establish SbC. BC's actions should not be considered as scripted in that he placed himself in a position to be shot. To the contrary, even if BC was contemplating SbC, the intervention of the police sniper does not fit logically into that plan at that moment in time.

A change of heart

The following case allows the reader to follow the progression of events that seemingly proceed along the lines of SbC only to change dramatically when the actor's focus is redirected. The case involves LA, a 37-year old, White female who after an alcohol fueled argument with her husband engages in behavior with the intention of provoking police officers into a deadly force encounter only to reconsider her options. The irony in this case was that LA's initial behavior was intended to be self-destructive, but her change of heart did not prevent her from being seriously wounded by a bullet fired from the gun of a police officer.

There is a single cover sheet that identifies the actor in this case as a female wishing that police officers respond and kill her in self-defense. There is no case study of this file and the file appears to be submitted based on LA's initial actions that prompted a police response.

> Police responded to a radio call of a possible psychotic woman with a shotgun or rifle acting in a bizarre manner.
>
> Officers were directed to the area of a residence behind a store where the call was first reported. As officers arrived they recognized the house as being the same house where they handled a disturbed person call involving a woman 40 minutes earlier.
>
> They observed a woman rapidly moving through the house. Other movement indicating the presence of others was not noted.
>
> The woman quickly exited the house and reportedly assumed a combat stance pointing at the officers with her arms extended.

The officers observed a dark object in her hands.

One officer fired a shot at her. She was struck and fell to the ground.

The interview of one of the officers involved reveals that the responding officers had no plan as how to approach the scene.

The officer had moved to a position of cover and recalls hearing other officers tracking the movement of the female. He hears the back door open rapidly and observes another officer crouch and fire his weapon.

This officer did not see the female at first until she fell to the ground after being shot.

He recalls the victim saying something to the effect, "I guess I just wanted to get shot."

The officer leaned over LA and questioned her about the location of the gun and she replied that she did not have a gun she had a coat hanger.

LA stated several times, "Who shot me? What's his name?" The officer questioned LA as to why she wanted to know who shot her and she replied "I just want to tell the officer it's not his fault."

As the officer was checking LA for injuries he detected the smell of alcohol on her breath. It was then that he noticed the coat hanger with a red and tan doily lying on the ground partially underneath LA.

A search of the area by the officers located the rifle. The location was plotted on the crime scene sketch and was in the carport adjacent to the porch were the shooting took place.

LA's husband was interviewed and relates the story about the police coming earlier at his request. He notes that he and LA had been drinking and that he felt she consumed a considerable number of beers, but describes her as a person who holds herself well when drinking. They had been arguing for about an hour and he believes the wife had been drinking since 5:00 p.m.

The husband informed the police that LA had called approximately one hour earlier and that the officers on scene were less than cordial and stayed for about three minutes before leaving.

After the police leave the first time they begin arguing again.

The husband did not remember LA leaving the premises prior to the incident. He was not paying her much attention at that point.

He did indicate that just moments prior to the shooting LA did get up from where she was sitting in the living room and go toward the kitchen. After that he recalls hearing a shot and went outside to investigate.

The husband was not surprised that his wife had been shot but could not offer any explanation as to what prompted her actions.

The couple's daughter was also interviewed. She was described by police as a hostile and antagonistic witness.

She knew her mother had been drinking but did not categorize her as being drunk and indicated she knew how her mother acted when she was drunk.

The daughter described the mother and father as arguing and being somewhat physical, pushing each other, but not physically fighting.

The daughter called the police after the parents began arguing again. She relates that she was specific in telling police not to show up with any guns. The problem with this statement is that there is nothing to indicate that she was aware that the mother was in any danger. This statement is after the fact and is more accusatory in nature.

The daughter never sees LA leave the house prior to the incident.

She is questioned about her mother's mental state. She states that her mother made a remark or comment to the effect that "one of these days, I'm going to kill myself" and that, "I'd do it tonight if I had the right equipment."

A check of the audio tapes of the phone call placed by a woman believed to be LA reveals the following statement: "I want you to send some police officers down to (**deleted**), so they can see what I'm going to do", or "what I'm about to do."

After the woman, believed to be LA, terminated the initial call her husband called back and inquired about the call his wife had just made. The police operator reports hearing a woman's voice in the background saying something to the effect, "Send the police. I demand that you send the police so they can see what I'm going to do."

The interview of LA was conducted at the hospital. The investigators informed LA that there were no charges pending against her and they were interested in learning from her what happened prior to the shooting. She replied that she was fed up with life and that her and her husband were experiencing severe marital problems. She was looking for the easy way out.

The investigator categorized LA as extremely depressed. LA had described to the investigator a pattern of what could be considered as abusive behavior by her husband.

When questioned as to why she took the gun to the outside in the area of the convenience store LA replied, "So the police would have to shoot me. I knew it (rifle) didn't work, but they would have to do it, wouldn't they?"

LA stated that her husband knew she had taken the rifle outside and that he had taken it away from her before the police arrived. She left by the back door because she did not want to have to pass her husband in the living room. She grabbed the hanger as she left the house because she was angry and wanted to strike something.

LA was not aware that the police were outside of her home when she exited, and it was not her intention or expectation at that time to be shot by the police.

LA stated to investigators, "Haven't you ever been so mad that you just wanted to strike out at something?" it was her intention of turning and striking the house when she exited the home. She recalls being shot at this point.

LA became aware, after the fact, that the police might have thought she had a gun. However, she does not connect that with SbC. "I know he (the officer) probably thought I had a gun."

LA states almost laughingly that the officer should get more training that he was not a very good shot.

The submitting officer classifies this as an attempted suicide, but offers no justification or supporting evidence. LA responds to officers questions as to why she ran out toward them in the manner that she did and she replies "I guess I just wanted to get shot." This statement appears to be the nexus for the classification of attempt suicide, but LA's statements in the hospital to investigators reveals a different state of mind. Her actions immediately preceding the shooting are not indicative of SbC.

It is probable to believe LA had suicidal ideation and may have formulated a plan indicative of SbC, but her actions at the time she was shot were expressive in nature and are not considered suicidal. There was a break in thought by LA. Perhaps after the acting out with the coat hanger she may have returned to argue more with he husband, to continue to drink, or even to go to bed. She did realize that her actions were perceived by police as threatening, and she is understanding of that, but her previous thoughts related to suicide and her actions do not appear to be linked to the actions that resulted in her being shot.

Following some bad advice

This case has the distinction of being the one case in the data set that could be classified as situation where a person was provoked into a course of action by police. Classifying this case as SbC justifies the argument presented by Fyfe (2004) that the phenomenon obfuscates sloppy police work with SbC.

The case study provides a detailed synopsis of the case that involved a 12-hour standoff between police and RR. The submitting officer also provides a thorough and comprehensive analysis of OT's state of mind, mental diagnosis and an opinion as to why OT's actions were considered suicidal. This analysis goes much deeper than any previous case studies examined. Yet the case study fails to recognize the deliberate provocation of OT pushing him into a fit of rage that culminates in his death. The case file is complimented with an extensive array of crime scene and media photographs allowing for a visual appreciation of the milieu, instrumentalities, and the actions of OT as he rushes at police in his final moments.

> OT is a diagnosed paranoid-schizophrenic who had stopped taking medication approximately one week prior to the present incident.
>
> Local mental health workers had responded to OT's home and requested police assistance based on a report from his mother that OT, a very large man (6'8" – 300), had threatened to first kill his mother and then kill himself.
>
> The mental health workers and police attempted to speak with OT who refused to allow them to enter the home. OT told them to leave his property or he would kill them. OT closed the door and a sound that was described as the action of a shotgun could be heard coming from inside. OT's mother was believed to be in the home at

this time, but it was later learned that the mother had called police from a location outside of the home.

A 12-hour standoff began.

OT had been previously committed to a state mental hospital. That incident required several officers to subdue and restrain OT who was a large, physical man. The mental health workers at the scene worked with police hostage negotiators to develop a profile of OT. This profile revealed that OT was:

- A diagnosed paranoid-schizophrenic;

- He had recently filed his teeth to points;

- He was a man who would follow through on what he said, good, or bad;

- He had a fondness for knives;

- He had not taken his medication in at least eight days;

- He had little if any sleep in the past three days;

- His frame of mind was not considered stable; and

- He was difficult to communicate with.

The incident had begun just before noon and would last well into the night ending just before 11:00 p.m. Early in the negotiations OT would keep conversations very short, often hanging up. At one point he stated, "You [police] are out to get me." He made statements regarding not taking any more of "your fucking medication," and that he would be taking his own medication now. The initial case study suggests that this statement was analogous to suicidal thoughts inferring that OT had developed a plan involving his death.

About five hours into the incident OT can be seen waving and smiling from inside the house. A local TV broadcast captures these images broadcasting them live. Although this point is not directly mentioned in police reports there is the inference that OT was watching the drama unfold on TV from within his home. A short time later the utilities to the house are turned off and it is obvious that OT is agitated by these actions.

The police recognize the need to maintain dialogue with OT and a decision was made to break a large window in the residence for the purpose of throwing in a telephone. This tactic is questioned considering the paranoid state that OT is in. By this point his mother is obviously safe and OT is only a threat to himself. The tactic was clearly designed to intimidate OT and establish police control of the scene. It

131

backfired. OT responded in an aggressive manner and broke the remaining portion of the window and somehow disabled the telephone.

At 10:00 p.m. OT exited the home and sat on the front porch. He could be heard shouting at the police and began banging the sidewalk in front of the home with a club. After 10 minutes of this OT went back inside of the home.

Officers were developing a strategy to coax OT back outside with an expectation of rushing him with SWAT officers in an attempt to take him into custody. Initial attempts to use food and offers to talk with family and clergy were unsuccessful.

A mental health worker advises the hostage negotiator that a course of action to consider based on OT's mental state and arrogance would be to challenge him and make him mad. The police were going to provoke OT in an attempt to force him into a trap. How sound was this logic?

The mental health worker advised police that OT would feel secure in his home and would not assist in efforts to leave the house. The house was OT's safety zone. The theory was that by forcing OT from the home he would lose the security of the house and overcoming him would be easier.

The mental health worker informed the negotiator that OT was found of the actor John Wayne and that he harbored a hatred for "preppies." The negotiator used this knowledge to verbally challenge OT. The negotiator played on OT's fondness of John Wayne and implied that he, the negotiator, was a preppie. The hostage negotiator jumped into this with both feet. OT's mind was fair game. The banter continued, and it worked. A short time later OT charged from the home armed with what appeared to be a club or pipe. OT's weaknesses were exploited and he reacted with what could best be described as blind rage. His objective was to attack the negotiator.

Moving quickly for a man of his size OT rapidly closed the distance between him and officers closest to the home. Less lethal means of force were an option, but OT's speed closed the distance too quickly. The proximity of OT to the less lethal system would surely result in a fatal wound. Officers used pepper spray, but OT continued to advance on two officers nearest to him. Was OT immune to the affects of pepper spray, or did the officers fail to hit the mark as this large, raging man rapidly approached their positions?

Both officers fired at OT as he closed the gap. OT died at a local hospital.

The autopsy report notes that OT had a slight laceration on the right side of his chest. This slight injury was believed to be self-inflicted.

OT's mother reported to police that OT had enough food to last him for 10 months. The crime scene investigation revealed that OT had taken considerable steps to barricade the home in an effort to prevent a police entry. This is not something that a person contemplating SbC would be inclined to do. Two revolvers were also found inside the home during the crime scene search.

Whatever OT's state of mind was during this incident it would appear that provoking the police into killing him was not a consideration. This point is significant considering that OT was preparing more defensively as opposed to considerations of offensive attacks against police.

A review of the file reveals that the police were clearly thinking of ways to psychologically outsmart OT. They considered breaching the door as a way of challenging his safety zone. They also considered the consequences of a failed action would cause OT to reinforce and further barricade himself. There is a single entry in one investigative report that notes the discussion by on-scene personnel of the possibility of this being SbC. However, there is no other supporting documentation or discussion in either the case file or the case study to justify this assertion. The police plan was clearly intended to agitate OT. When OT emerged from the house he was heard saying that he was going to "kill him." Ostensibly, OT was speaking about the hostage negotiator.

There was an on-scene discussion regarding a police withdrawal from the area since OT had not committed a felony up until that point. The concurrence among those present during the incident was that withdrawal was not an option since there was an emergent detention order that had been issued for OT and his violent nature.

This case is well analyzed by the submitting officer. However, what is viewed as suicidal behavior on OT's part by running from the home toward police officers in a threatening manner is more likely a response to the antagonism of the hostage negotiator. The reaction of OT to this antagonism was not a well thought out consideration by police or the mental health worker. There is no indication that the hostage negotiator or the mental health

133

worker considered that OT would become so enraged that he would blindly try to kill the hostage negotiator or anyone else for that matter.

This case, and others like it, is a clear example of how the phenomenon of SbC is obviously misunderstood and improperly applied, and therefore lends credence to two very legitimate points; One point is the valid criticism of the lack of a clear definition of SbC. A second point in this regard would question the reliability and validity of existing data on the prevalence of SbC cases without benefit of a standardized definition. The following case exemplifies the exclusion of a case when one or more definitional criteria are absent.

A running gun battle

This case involves CM a 25-year old, white male. CM's actions leading up and during this incident are filled with anger, raw emotion, self-destructive behavior, and violence. CM was diagnosed as Bi-Polar Manic Depressive. He had recently stopped taking his medication and was abusing alcohol and marijuana, actions that likely caused him to be fired from his job as a laborer. CM's relationship with his girlfriend was described as being rocky over the past several months.

The dramatic events of a running gun battle with police are the culmination of extremely violent events involving CM. What is absent is any form or type of communication related to suicidal ideation or action(s). The case study provides a detailed overview of the case, and is one of a limited number of exceptional case studies that focus on the actor as well as their actions.

> The incident begins in the early morning hours with CM packing his car with two shotguns. A friend describes CM as being in a state of panic. CM's girlfriend described his moods as going from very threatening one moment to apologetic the

next. One person described CM as hating everyone and that he wanted to kill everyone.

The friend observed CM writing on one of the shotguns with some type of marker. He thought CM wrote something about "Cops Ass". In fact he wrote " Fukin Pigz Az" on one side of the weapon and "187" on the opposite side. The number 187 in local jargon represented the word murder.

CM left a note for a friend allowing for the friend to have his car in the event that something was to happen to him. What could happen to CM? What was he planning? Did he expect something to happen?

A triggering event may have occurred three days before the incident when CM attempted to purchase a gift for his mother for Mother's Day that was just two days away. CM tried to pay for the purchase with a check but the sales clerk refused to accept the check. CM became enraged. He threatened the clerk with a knife. CM left the store without hurting the clerk. Many of CM's friends described this incident has having a profound effect on CM.

On the morning of the incident CM demanded money from his girlfriend before leaving the house. At one point CM considered taking his girlfriend as a hostage, but why? CM changed his mind. He told her that she was the only person who had ever loved him. CM took some money from his girlfriend and left.

CM then went on a wild one-man crime spree. Pulling up to a small store at 6:00 a.m. he entered with a shotgun demanding money. Before fleeing the store CM fired the shotgun into the ceiling. As he fled the area CM began randomly shooting at passing motorists.

Ten minutes later local police spot CM's vehicle. CM fires at the passing police car and a pursuit, at times punctuated with a running gun battle, began.

CM losses control of his car and the vehicle stops in a parking lot. CM continues to engage the police in gunfire from outside of the car. He can be seen moving around the exterior of car, but it was not clear what he was doing. The shooting stops and at one point CM complies with police commands to raise his hands. That would not last.

CM can be seen suddenly dropping his hands as he moved toward the open driver's side door of his car. Officers could see that CM had grabbed something from inside of the car. CM began running at the officers. His hands were in front of him, at waist level, holding something.

CM was closing the gap between him and the officers. What was CM holding? Was it a gun, a weapon of some sort? The advantages of time and distance were rapidly closing. CM was an immediate threat. The police reacted with deadly force.

The object in CM's hands was found to be a can opener.

The case study examines CM's profile with sufficient detail. CM's past and present behavior is closely scrutinized. The submitting officer notes that CM exhibited fear, suspicion, paranoia, and often reacted to situations with anger, and takes the extraordinary step in suggesting these responses are often associated with other types of mental illness. In drawing the parallel between CM's behavior and Antisocial Personality Disorder the submitting officer suggests that CM's behavior placed him at increased risk for suicide and the potential for dying in a violent manner. All of this helps to portray a clear portrait of CM. Where the analysis is limited is the absence of an examination of CM's actions that resulted in his death, and any nexus that these actions have in classifying the case as SbC.

CM initiated the course of events that resulted in his death. His actions seemingly were voluntary. Just what was his intent at that moment, and more importantly was he capable of forming that intent? An *ex post facto* answer to these questions is difficult at best. What is more relevant to this research is the question; can this case be classified as SbC? CM entered the final act in the script armed with nothing more than a can opener. The dynamics of this incident were highly volatile and fast paced. The officers perceived CM's actions in advancing on them as threatening. What is missing is any type or form of communication from CM that he was suicidal. From a subjective standpoint it can be argued that his actions were clearly suicidal. The problem with an assessment like is that it reinforces the legitimate criticism of SbC in failing to adhere to or follow objective criteria. For that reason, this case was excluded from the final data set.

Hearing voices

The following case is emblematic of the myopia that occurs in viewing SbC through the actions of a person as the determinate for classification at the expense of excluding the cognition of the actor. Although the submitting officer was required to sanitize this case for legal reasons, deleting certain case related information, sufficient personal information about the actor was obtained allowing for a thorough secondary analysis.

The case involves AA a 46-year old, Black male. The identity of the actor could not be determined. A random selection of initials is used for ease of relating the facts of the case.

AA was a military veteran with a history of medical and psychological disorders that led to his removal from active service. At the time of his discharge during the Viet Nam War he was diagnosed with depression. When asked about his illness AA will tell people that he is diagnosed with Posttraumatic Stress Disorder (PTSD).

AA exhibited a pattern of behavior in and around his home that was often times described as irrational. Living near a large military base he would frequent the facility for legitimate reasons associated with on-going medical care. However, several incidences prior to his death involved harassing and threatening behavior aimed at neighbors and military personnel that he would come into contact with. Neighbors described the subject as having mental problems and that he would do and say strange things. It was believed that AA would at times hallucinate. He was described in previous police reports as a person who was "mentally unstable."

AA would tell almost anyone who would listen that he heard voices in his head and that the voices were coming from communications equipment located nearby on the military base.

Police reports indicate that AA, notwithstanding his diagnosed and observed mental state, was able to purchase a handgun prior to the incident and reportedly test fired the weapon in his backyard.

On the day of the incident AA informed his father that he was "going to straighten out his head and get the moon and the stars out of his head." AA then left his house. Soon thereafter he entered the military installation, using a legitimate veteran's identification card, and proceeded to a building where he discharged the handgun several times. He then proceeded to an office and demanded entrance to a secure area.

It appears that AA is seeking to find the source of the voices he hears in his head. He stated he would "pop someone" if they did not open the door. In that room is a person that AA does not know, and who has no bearing on AA's life other than being present at that moment with AA.

In a fateful move the occupant of the room attempts to leave, an act that prompts AA to kill him.

Base security personnel responded to the report of shots fired and encountered AA on a second floor landing. One of the officers spoke with AA in an attempt to calm him down. AA's response appears to be delusional. He does not make any sense in what he is saying or referring to.

AA was aware that he had killed someone and that that person was bleeding. His actions toward the security officer that he was speaking with were perceived as non-threatening.

In a surprising and gutsy move the officer at one-point lowers his weapon and shows AA that he does not intend to harm him.

AA's response to this was as equally surprising. AA turned his attention toward another officer and fires his gun. AA then turns back toward the original officer with the gun pointed at him. The officer shoots and kills him.

AA's actions were not that of a rational person. There is a documented history of

significant mental illness. The reports from family, neighbors, base personnel, and the local

police were that he was a man who was not in a right frame of mind. There were the reports

of hallucinations. Voices. Diagnosed mental illness. All of these factors seriously question

AA's sanity.

The preliminary review of the initial case study did not uncover any evidence that would

support a classification of SbC. A more thorough secondary analysis failed to find anything

to suggest that AA was suicidal, had communicated any type of suicidal intent, or that his

actions were linked in any way to an expectation or a desire to die.

Overall, it has been shown in the present analysis that excluded cases have a common denominator; the submitting officers have focused their analysis on actions at the expense of other situational or demographic variables. The cause for these gaps is rooted in the lack of standardization of any definition of what SbC is, or is not, and it is the bridging of these knowledge gaps that will be discussed in detail in the final chapter of this report.

DEMOGRAPHIC AND SITUATIONAL VARIABLES

This study was constructed as an exploratory qualitative analysis relying on a collective case study methodology. As such, the general research design was not intended for the purpose of conducting statistical analysis. However, the richness of the data, and the ability to capture it undiluted, presented an opportunity to expand the scope of the research by collecting descriptive statistics of this data and comparing it with data from other studies of SbC. Additionally, these variables help to develop a better understanding of what common threads are likely to exist in SbC cases.

This next section will discuss demographic and situational variables that were found in each of the included cases (N=26). Using SPSS, the variables for the most part will be presented and discussed in the form of frequency distributions and where appropriate compared to other studies found in the literature. In the case of situational variables recording the continuum of force used by police officers the data will be compared using bar graphs allowing for the visual comparison of the recorded frequencies.

Gender

The gender analysis was computed as a frequency of the total N=26 of included cases. The percentage distribution reveals a substantial variation between males, 88.5 %, and females 11.5 %.

Table 8: Gender

0=female, 1=male

		Frequency	Percent	Valid Percent	Cumulative Percent
Valid	0	3	11.5	11.5	11.5
	1	23	88.5	88.5	100.0
	Total	26	100.0	100.0	

Race

The variable race was coded in accordance with national standards for police in recording victim and suspect information. The majority of the cases, 76.9 %, involved people who were classified in the police reports as White. Hispanics and Blacks each accounted for significantly less numbers of the total with 11.5 % of the cases.

Table 9: Race

1=asian, 2=black, 3=hisp, 4=white, 5=Native

		Frequency	Percent	Valid	Cumulative Percent
Valid	2	3	11.5	11.5	11.5
	3	3	11.5	11.5	23.1
	4	20	76.9	76.9	100.0
	Total	26	100.0	100.0	

Age

The variable age was examined to determine range as well as frequency. The range in age spanned from the youngest person being 20-years of age and the oldest being 76. The mean age for this cohort was 36.92. The single highest frequency for age was 47-years of age with a total of three cases, or 11.5 %, and a crosstabulation analysis revealed that each of these were male. This was followed by five cases with a frequency of two. Single representations of age occurred in 13 of the cases.

Table 10: Age

Descriptive Statistics

	N	Minimum	Maximum	Mean	Std. Deviation
AGE	26	20	76	36.92	13.251
Valid N (listwise)	26				

Criminal History

This variable was created in an effort to determine what number of cases, if any, involved a person with a criminal history involving a conviction. This information was obtained from the police reports in 84.6 % of the cases. Four cases, 15.4 %, did not contain sufficient information to determine if a criminal history existed. In four cases, 34.6 %, there was no report or indication of a criminal history.

The interest here, although not directly related to this research, would be to see if there is any possibility of this individual variable having a predictive value in relation to future research on SbC. Based on the results generated in this study it is obvious there is not an overwhelming majority of cases involving a past criminal history. Another factor that is equally as problematic in this regard was that not all of the case files contained sufficient information that allowed for the establishment of the range and type of cases. Future examination of the relationship, if any exists, between criminal history and SbC will require data that contains or is designed to record the relevant information.

Table 11: Criminal History

0=no, 1=yes, 999=unknown

		Frequency	Percent	Valid Percent	Cumulative Percent
Valid	0	9	34.6	34.6	34.6
	1	13	50.0	50.0	84.6
	999	4	15.4	15.4	100.0
	Total	26	100.0	100.0	

Marital Status

The demographic variable related to marital status was coded based on five possibilities; not married, married, separated, divorced, and widow/widower. The vast majority of the cases, or 46.2 % (n=12), involved persons who were not married, which was more than double than those individuals who were married accounting for 19.2 % (n=5). The downward trend continues with separations accounting for 11.5 % (n=3), followed by divorced and widow/widower each occurring in 3.8 % (n=1) of the cases. Four of the cases (15.4%) did not contain sufficient information to determine marital status.

Table 12: Marital Status

0=no, 1=marry, 2=separate, 3=div, 4=wid

		Frequency	Percent	Valid Percent	Cumulative Percent
Valid	0	12	46.2	46.2	46.2
	1	5	19.2	19.2	65.4
	2	3	11.5	11.5	76.9
	3	1	3.8	3.8	80.8
	4	1	3.8	3.8	84.6
	999	4	15.4	15.4	100.0
	Total	26	100.0	100.0	

Time

In attempting to record the time of each incident there were significant gaps in information. This variable accounts for the largest percentage, 30.8%, of missing data (n=8). The

142

interest in determining a temporal span of the incident is an effort to view the range of time, and if that range allows for any chance of generalization. Time was recorded using the SPSS format *hh:mm:ss*.

The examination of the data output for this variable is very revealing. The range is extreme, a polarization. The shortest period of time, occurring once in this data set, took just 15 seconds from beginning to end. On the other end of the spectrum is a single incident spanning the course of 20 hours! Between these polar opposites are 16 cases ranging from one minute to 10 hours. Overall, the majority of cases (n=10) exceed one hour in duration, a factor that is in need of further quantitative examination. If future research can show a nexus between time and SbC the considerations for a police response to these types of incidents can be examined further with an eye toward mitigation and other less lethal options.

Table 13: Time Span of SbC Incident

Time

		Frequency	Percent	Valid Percent	Cumulative Percent
Valid	0:00:15	1	3.8	5.6	5.6
	0:01:00	2	7.7	11.1	16.7
	0:04:00	1	3.8	5.6	22.2
	0:05:00	1	3.8	5.6	27.8
	0:10:00	1	3.8	5.6	33.3
	0:15:00	1	3.8	5.6	38.9
	0:50:00	1	3.8	5.6	44.4
	1:18:00	1	3.8	5.6	50.0
	1:20:00	1	3.8	5.6	55.6
	2:14:00	1	3.8	5.6	61.1
	2:38:00	1	3.8	5.6	66.7
	2:48:00	1	3.8	5.6	72.2
	2:55:00	1	3.8	5.6	77.8
	3:00:00	1	3.8	5.6	83.3
	3:45:00	1	3.8	5.6	88.9
	10:00:00	1	3.8	5.6	94.4
	20:00:00	1	3.8	5.6	100.0
	Total	18	69.2	100.0	
Missing	System	8	30.8		
Total		26	100.0		

143

Domestic violence

Domestic violence is a source of significant life stressors for all parties involved, the victim(s) as well as the offending party. This variable was created in an attempt to see how many, if any, SbC cases originated with domestic violence cases. For the purpose of this study the initial police report(s) found in the case files are what determined the presence of domestic violence. Domestic violence was coded simply as present or not. The many facets of domestic violence offenses were not coded due to a significant absence of information in the case files.

The vast majority, 73.1 % (n=19), of the data did not originate from domestic violence cases. Those cases that did involve some level or type of domestic violence were significantly less with 26.9 % (n=7) as shown in Table 7.

Crime

As with the variable time, there were significant gaps in information regarding the commission of a crime, as a precipitating or preceding event to SbC. SbC as an act is criminal in nature. An actor provokes a police officer into the use of deadly force. The provocation itself involves a level of criminality that is determined by the nature and extent of a threat or use of force against the police or a third party. Differentiating between what was a crime and an offense, or a felony and a misdemeanor, was difficult. The police reports varied in the depth of information that was contained, or missing. Many of the criminal acts were obvious, others more obscure.

Using a case summary analysis of the occurrence of crime and the typology it was determined that nine of the 10 cases involving the commission of crime involved a felony.

Table 14: Occurrence of Crime

0=no, 1=yes

		Frequency	Percent	Valid Percent	Cumulative Percent
Valid	0	16	61.5	61.5	61.5
	1	10	38.5	38.5	100.0
	Total	26	100.0	100.0	

Communicating suicidal ideation

This section examines three separate variables focusing on the existence of evidence revealing the communication of any type, verbal or nonverbal, of suicidal ideation, including the presence of a suicide note(s). The single variable of communication is a significant factor in determining whether or not a case would be included or excluded. The definitional criterion for this research requires that evidence of communication is present. Inclusion of a case required evidence that showed some type of communication exists, before, during, or in some cases after an SbC incident. In all but one of the cases this evidence was easily recognizable. One case required in-depth analysis of statements made by the actor to family and mental health workers to uncover a series of verbal communications exposing a plan of SbC. Overall, all included cases, as shown in Table 15, contained sufficient evidence that demonstrated some form of communication by the suicidal actor.

Communicating suicidal ideation is not limited to just the spoken word. The use of gestures to convey intention or ideation in the suicidal drama is not something new. Table 16 reveals that non-verbal communication was identified in 30.8 % (n=8) of the included cases. Examples of non-verbal communication that were noted in this research include the

145

placing or pointing of a firearm(s) at the body/head, similarly the use of an edged weapon, and/or mimicking a violent act by simulating the use of a weapon with an empty hand.

Another form of communication involving suicide and suicide ideation is the use of a written note, and is listed in Table 17. In only 7.7 % of the cases (n=2) a suicide note was left or found. In one of these cases a total of nine notes were left including one to the officer that was involved.[29]

Table 15: Communicating Suicidal Ideation

Communication 0=no, 1=yes

		Frequency	Percent	Valid Percent	Cumulative Percent
Valid	1	26	100.0	100.0	100.0

Table 16: Non-verbal Communication

0=no, 1=yes

		Frequency	Percent	Valid Percent	Cumulative Percent
Valid	0	18	69.2	69.2	69.2
	1	8	30.8	30.8	100.0
	Total	26	100.0	100.0	

Table 17: Suicide Note(s)

0=no, 1=yes

		Frequency	Percent	Valid Percent	Cumulative Percent
Valid	0	24	92.3	92.3	92.3
	1	2	7.7	7.7	100.0
	Total	26	100.0	100.0	

---

[29] Due to the delimitation not allowing for identifying any person in these case files this case was purposely not discussed in the analysis.

Police involvement

The actions and reactions of the police in SbC incidents is an integral part of these dramas. Although this research is primarily focused on the suicidal actor the ability to capture and record certain aspects of police involvement is too invaluable an opportunity to overlook. Two variables that were examined in this regard were focused on the use of cover by police officers in response to the actions of the actor and the element of surprise that the actor was able to exploit. Cover as opposed to concealment offers some level of protection against attack while concealment offers little if any security against attack. In constructing a variable to measure if the actions of the actor surprised the responding officers it was necessary to make an objective determination based on the facts contained in the original police files.

In Table 18 the analysis reveals that in 61.5 % of the cases (n=16) the police were capable of using cover in an attempt to protect themselves. The type and frequency of cover is shown in Table 19. The use of a police vehicle was the most frequent type of cover with 42.3 % (n=11) and the use of some from or type of structure as cover occurred in 19.2 % (n=5) of the cases. The element of surprise occurred less frequently than may be expected given the nature of SbC. Table 20 shows that police were aware of a threat in 57.7 % (n=15) of the cases.

A Crosstab analysis was conducted in an attempt to determine the use of cover in relation to the existence of surprise. Table 21 illustrates the variance between the use of cover and surprise. By a ratio of more than 2:1 cover is used when surprise is not a factor.

Table 18: Police Use of Cover

Cover 0=no, 1=yes

		Frequency	Percent	Valid Percent	Cumulative Percent
Valid	0	10	38.5	38.5	38.5
	1	16	61.5	61.5	100.0
	Total	26	100.0	100.0	

Table 19: Type of Cover

1=car, 2=structure, 3=none

		Frequency	Percent	Valid Percent	Cumulative Percent
Valid	1	11	42.3	45.8	45.8
	2	5	19.2	20.8	66.7
	3	8	30.8	33.3	100.0
	Total	24	92.3	100.0	
Missing	System	2	7.7		
Total		26	100.0		

Table 20: Surprise Movement/Attack

Suprise 0=no, 1=yes

		Frequency	Percent	Valid Percent	Cumulative Percent
Valid	0	15	57.7	57.7	57.7
	1	11	42.3	42.3	100.0
	Total	26	100.0	100.0	

Table 21: Use of Cover – Surprise Movement/Attack

Cover 0=no, 1=yes * Suprise 0=no, 1=yes Crosstabulation

Count

		Suprise 0=no, 1=yes		Total
		0	1	
Cover 0=no, 1=yes	0	4	6	10
	1	11	5	16
Total		15	11	26

Family

The presence of family members at SbC incidents, as depicted in Table 22, was slightly less in frequency occurring 46.2 % of the time (n=12) compared to the remaining 53.8 % of the cases (n=14) when family members were not present.

Table 22: Presence of Family Members

Family 0=no, 1=yes

		Frequency	Percent	Valid Percent	Cumulative Percent
Valid	0	14	53.8	53.8	53.8
	1	12	46.2	46.2	100.0
	Total	26	100.0	100.0	

Location of Incident

In selecting variables dealing with the possible location of SbC incidents the three most common sites noted during the preliminary review of the data were utilized. Motor vehicles were involved in 19.2 % of the cases (n=5) as shown in Table 23. The home or residence of the actor or another victim occurred with greater frequency as noted in Table 24. In 53.8 % of the cases the SbC played out in or around a residence. Table 25 reveals that only 7.7 % (n=2) of the cases occurred at the work place.

A Crosstabulation of the variables family and location as depicted in Table 26 reveals that the majority of time an incident occurs in or proximate to the home a family member was present. Ten of the 14 cases occurring in or near the home were found to have family members present.

Table 23: Motor Vehicle

MV 0=no, 1=yes

		Frequency	Percent	Valid Percent	Cumulative Percent
Valid	0	21	80.8	80.8	80.8
	1	5	19.2	19.2	100.0
	Total	26	100.0	100.0	

Table 24: Home/Residence

Home 0=no, 1=yes

		Frequency	Percent	Valid Percent	Cumulative Percent
Valid	0	12	46.2	46.2	46.2
	1	14	53.8	53.8	100.0
	Total	26	100.0	100.0	

Table 25: Work

Work 0=no, 1=yes

		Frequency	Percent	Valid Percent	Cumulative Percent
Valid	0	24	92.3	92.3	92.3
	1	2	7.7	7.7	100.0
	Total	26	100.0	100.0	

Table 26: Crosstab Analysis

Home 0=no, 1=yes * Family 0=no, 1=yes Crosstabulation

Count

		Family 0=no, 1=yes		Total
		0	1	
Home 0=no, 1=yes	0	10	2	12
	1	4	10	14
Total		14	12	26

Alcohol and Drugs

The use of alcohol in SbC incidents examined in this study far exceeded the use of drugs and/or a combination of the two. In 61.5 % of the cases, as shown in Table 27, the use of alcohol was clearly evident.

Drugs were less likely to be a factor in many of these cases as seen in Table 28. In 15.4 % of the cases (n=4) there was obvious evidence of drug use. The combined use of drugs and alcohol, as depicted in Table 29, occurred in 11.5 % of the cases (n=3).

Although many of the case files contained some type of toxicology report identifying the presence of alcohol or drugs in the actor's system the need to rely solely on these reports for this information was not necessary.

Table 27: Alcohol

Alcohol 0=no, 1=yes, 2=tox, 999=unknown

		Frequency	Percent	Valid Percent	Cumulative Percent
Valid	0	10	38.5	38.5	38.5
	1	16	61.5	61.5	100.0
	Total	26	100.0	100.0	

Table 28: Drugs

Drugs 0=no, 1=yes, 2=tox, 999=unknown

		Frequency	Percent	Valid Percent	Cumulative Percent
Valid	0	19	73.1	82.6	82.6
	1	4	15.4	17.4	100.0
	Total	23	88.5	100.0	
Missing	System	3	11.5		
Total		26	100.0		

Table 29: Alcohol/Drug Use Combined

PolyAbuse 0=no, 1=yes, 2=tox, 999=unknown

		Frequency	Percent	Valid Percent	Cumulative Percent
Valid	0	20	76.9	87.0	87.0
	1	3	11.5	13.0	100.0
	Total	23	88.5	100.0	
Missing	System	3	11.5		
Total		26	100.0		

Suicide Attempts

As with previous variables the examination of the existence of suicide attempts and the number of attempts is not adequately reported due to significant gaps in available information in the original police files. In examining a history of attempts involving the suicidal actor the data revealed that previous suicide attempts existed in 34.6 % of the cases (n=9). Table 30 reflects the dispersion between reported suicide attempts, the absence of attempts, and cases where it was unknown if an attempt had occurred.

Table 31 depicts the number of attempts, if any, that were identified in any of the cases. A single attempt occurred more frequently, occurring 26.9 % of time (n=7), than no attempt, with 23.1 % (n=6), or the one case (7.1%) documenting two previous attempts.

Table 30: Previous Suicide Attempts

Attempts 0=no, 1=yes,

		Frequency	Percent	Valid Percent	Cumulative Percent
Valid	0	9	34.6	34.6	34.6
	1	9	34.6	34.6	69.2
	999	8	30.8	30.8	100.0
	Total	26	100.0	100.0	

Table 31: Number of Attempts

Number Attempts

		Frequency	Percent	Valid Percent	Cumulative Percent
Valid	0	6	23.1	42.9	42.9
	1	7	26.9	50.0	92.9
	2	1	3.8	7.1	100.0
	Total	14	53.8	100.0	
Missing	System	12	46.2		
Total		26	100.0		

Psychiatric History

The presence of any psychiatric history was identified through references found within the original police files. These references were then crosschecked with additional references or evidence of past or current psychiatric care or referral found in the case studies. Cases that did not support the ability to crosscheck information were entered as unknowns. The vast majority, 65.4 % (n=17) of the cases, as shown in Table 32, contained sufficient evidence to support the existence of some type of psychiatric history. In Table 33 evidence of a legitimate diagnosis of mental illness also occurred in 65.4 % of the cases (n=17). The utility of this information is limited by the inability to list and compare the range of diagnosis of mental illness in each of these cases. However, in many cases (34.6%) the actual diagnosis was missing from the case file and the variable was coded 999=missing. One recurring diagnosis in the majority of the cases was often some form of depression.

Table 32: Evidence of Psychiatric History

Psychiatric History 0=no, 1=yes, 999=unknown

		Frequency	Percent	Valid Percent	Cumulative Percent
Valid	0	1	3.8	3.8	3.8
	1	17	65.4	65.4	69.2
	999	8	30.8	30.8	100.0
	Total	26	100.0	100.0	

153

Table 33: Medical Diagnosis

Diagnosis 0=no, 1=yes, 999=unknown

		Frequency	Percent	Valid Percent	Cumulative Percent
Valid	1	17	65.4	65.4	65.4
	999	9	34.6	34.6	100.0
	Total	26	100.0	100.0	

Weapons

The use and threat of weapons is a significant factor in SbC cases. The presence or perception of weapons is critical to the anticipated or expected response of police. Table 34 shows that weapons of one sort or another were visible at some point prior to the culmination of an SbC incident in 92.3 % of the cases (n=24). In just two cases the actor intimated the use or possession of a weapon. Similarly, Table 35 reveals that the threat to use a weapon or the display of a weapon in a threatening manner occurred 92.3 % of the time.

Table 34: Weapon

Weapon 0=no, 1=yes,

		Frequency	Percent	Valid Percent	Cumulative Percent
Valid	0	2	7.7	7.7	7.7
	1	24	92.3	92.3	100.0
	Total	26	100.0	100.0	

Table 35: Threat to Use Weapon

Threat 0=no, 1=yes,

		Frequency	Percent	Valid Percent	Cumulative Percent
Valid	0	2	7.7	7.7	7.7
	1	24	92.3	92.3	100.0
	Total	26	100.0	100.0	

Firearms

The use of firearms is the predominate choice of weapon in SbC cases. As seen in Table 36 firearms are used 65.4 % of the time (n=17), almost double the incidence of the use of other weapons. Table 37 shows the frequency of the various types of firearms that were used in the cases examined in this study. Handgun use occurred 46.2 % of the time (n=12) followed by the use of a shotgun in 19.2 % of the cases (n=5).

Table 36: Firearm

Firearm 0=no, 1=yes,

		Frequency	Percent	Valid Percent	Cumulative Percent
Valid	0	9	34.6	34.6	34.6
	1	17	65.4	65.4	100.0
	Total	26	100.0	100.0	

Table 37: Type of Firearm

Type 0=handgun, 1=rifle, 2=shotgun, 3=reptoy, 4=BB, 5=multiple,

		Frequency	Percent	Valid Percent	Cumulative Percent
Valid	0	12	46.2	57.1	57.1
	1	2	7.7	9.5	66.7
	2	5	19.2	23.8	90.5
	4	1	3.8	4.8	95.2
	5	1	3.8	4.8	100.0
	Total	21	80.8	100.0	
Missing	System	5	19.2		
Total		26	100.0		

The Use of Force Continuum

This section examines the continuum of force used by police in response to threat situations that can occur in SbC incidents. This variable is a construct of a generalized model depicting the gradation of five separate stages in the continuum. The first stage involves constructive use of force. The presence of officers and the verbalization of commands by those officers constitute a constructive use of force. The second stage in the continuum,

155

physical contact, involves incidences where officers use limited contact such as the placing of a hand on the suspect in an effort to control the suspect and the situation. Physical force is the third stage and includes various applications of force including but not limited to strikes, holds, and similar offensive or defensive maneuvers. The fourth stage, mechanical force, involves the use of impact weapons such as batons and clubs. Many jurisdictions also include chemical irritants in this category. As needed, officers are authorized to use acceptable levels of mechanical force if other less forceful measures prove ineffective or inefficient. The final stage in the continuum is deadly force. Less lethal weapons are included in this category due to the potential for lethality.

The graph in Table 38 depicts the disparity in the various stages in the continuum. All cases (N=26) involved some level of constructive force that was used by the police officer(s) that was present. In Table 39 the total number of cases involving the use of deadly force drops by one (n=25) since this case was an attempt and deadly force was not used. What is obvious in examining the graph in Table 38 is that the middle stages of the continuum are underrepresented in comparison to the first and last level. The explanation for this disparity is rooted in a qualitative analysis of the case files. SbC incidents are dynamic and fluid events and the options to use force are influenced by several demographic and situational variables. An expectation for any use of force incident to logically follow each and every step in a consecutive and uninterrupted flow is unrealistic. As with other variables in this study future evaluations are necessary. One recommendation is to consider examining the use of force continuum in other police use of force incidents and then compare those cases with confirmed cases of SbC.

Table 38: Use of Force Continuum

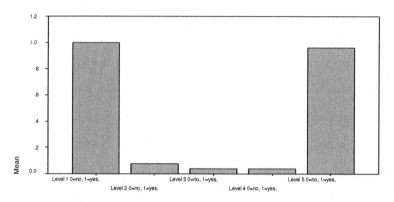

Table 39: Deadly Force

Level 5 0=no, 1=yes,

		Frequency	Percent	Valid Percent	Cumulative Percent
Valid	0	1	3.8	3.8	3.8
	1	25	96.2	96.2	100.0
	Total	26	100.0	100.0	

Scripted Behavior

Each of the included cases was examined for evidence of scripted behavior on the part of the suicidal actor. Scripted behavior for the purpose of this research is a construct used to describe the cause and effect actions of a suicidal actor in anticipation and/or response to the actions or inactions of police officers. When a suicidal actor enters the SbC drama and obviously presents or is perceived to present a threat the police officer(s) is expected to react accordingly. If the actions/reactions of that officer(s) does not produce the desired outcome through the use of deadly force the drama will expand.

157

The case studies presented in this research are representative of a small number of examples of how scripted behavior is evident in SbC. In the case of CO there was more than one instance of how he was attempting to achieve the desired end-state of SbC through obvious and stated intentions. The illumination of his head to allow for a clear shot by police, the repeated pointing of a handgun at the police, and finally his advancement on police officers resulted in the use of deadly force. The actions of TC were similarly intended to provoke a deadly force response by police. His quick and unexpected movements were choreographed to simulate the production of a weapon of some sort. A final example in this regard was the case involving CC. In this case CC was clear in his expectations. By firing a weapon in the presence of police officers CC intended to provoke a deadly force response. Failing to achieve this desired end-state he continued with a course of action eventually achieving his goal; SbC.

As a part of the necessary criteria for inclusion in the final data set scripted behavior is understandably present in each of the cases found in the final N=26. What is equally as important is the fact that scripted behavior was not found in a substantial number of the original N=61. Table 41 shows that 16.4 % of the cases (n=10) failed to meet the criteria for scripted behavior, and another 21.3 % of those cases (n=13) were excluded for methodological reasons. After final analysis of the remaining 59.0 % of the cases (n=36) determined that the total number of cases that clearly can be classified as SbC was further reduced to the final N=26, or 42.6 % of the original data set (N=61).

Table 40: Scripted Behavior – Included Cases

Scripted Behavior 0=no, 1=yes

		Frequency	Percent	Valid Percent	Cumulative Percent
Valid	1	26	100.0	100.0	100.0

Table 41: Preliminary Examination of Scripted Behavior

0=no, 1=yes, 2= excluded

		Frequency	Percent	Valid Percent	Cumulative Percent
Valid	0	10	16.4	16.9	16.9
	1	36	59.0	61.0	78.0
	2	13	21.3	22.0	100.0
	Total	59	96.7	100.0	
Missing	System	2	3.3		
Total		61	100.0		

Having established that scripted behavior of the suicidal actor is discernable and therefore measurable the suggestion to refine the term suicide-by-cop to a more accurate idiom would be logical. *Victim-scripted suicide* differentiates from SbC by establishing that the cause for the suicide lies with the suicidal actor and not the police officer.

Mode of Death

The final variable to be examined in this section identifies the mode of death (MOD). Table 42 lists the six categories found in the files that were reviewed in the final analysis. Due to gaps in information in the original police files in 11.5 % of the cases (n=3) the MOD could not be determined. This is due in large part to continuing police investigations, pending autopsy reports, or legal proceedings that had not yet been completed before the case study was conducted. Homicide was the most frequent MOD with 73.1 % of the cases (n=19)

159

being classified as such. Suicide and accident were not recorded in any of the cases in the

final N=26. The percentage of attempts accounted for 11.5 % (n=3). One case was clearly

labeled as pending without benefit of further explanation.

Table 41: Mode of Death

MOD 0=not determined, 1=homicide, 2=suicide, 3=accident, 4=attempt,
5=pending invest,

		Frequency	Percent	Valid Percent	Cumulative Percent
Valid	0	3	11.5	11.5	11.5
	1	19	73.1	73.1	84.6
	4	3	11.5	11.5	96.2
	5	1	3.8	3.8	100.0
	Total	26	100.0	100.0	

CHAPTER 6

This study has examined specific and distinct aspects of the SbC drama through the use of

a collective case study analysis for the purpose of developing a clearer understanding of

how the phenomenon is viewed by police practitioners. Additionally, two subordinate

examinations of the dynamics of SbC incidents, specifically the behavior of the suicidal

actor in relation to the response of police and the collection of data regarding demographic

and situational variables occurring in these incidents were also completed.

The initial conceptualization of this research proceeded with the expectation that cases

found within the original data set would provide sufficient information that would support

the SbC phenomenon. The nature of the original data set, which was a convenience sample

of independent case studies classified as SbC, was a significant factor in determining the

focus and design for this research. Each of the original case studies represented an

individual perspective of SbC, a perspective that was bounded by the understanding of the

phenomenon by each of the practitioners, and by facts of the particular case that was under

examination.

Using a two-pronged approach the research first developed a tripartite definition of SbC

delineating three distinct elements that must be present and can be clearly identified. SbC,

for the purpose of this research, has been defined as: An incident involving the use of

deadly force by a law enforcement agent(s) in response to the provocation of a threat/use of

deadly force against the agent(s) or others by an actor who has voluntarily entered the

suicidal drama and has communicated verbally or nonverbally the desire to commit suicide.

Second, a conceptual model of SbC was developed through a secondary analysis of individual case studies of police-involved shootings that were classified as SbC in the preliminary studies. The secondary analysis, and subsequent classification of a case(s) as SbC, required that the case file contain sufficient information regarding the actions of the suicidal actor that supported the classification through the definitional litmus developed for this research.

In the final analysis of the data this research determined that a majority of the original cases (N=57) that were originally classified as SbC did not meet the definitional criteria developed for this study, and a primary factor in many of these misclassifications was based on the erroneous assumption that the *actions* of the suicidal actor was the sole or principal determinant. Overall, less than half (45%) of the cases examined in the final analysis were classified as SbC. However, in each of the 26 cases that met the definitional criteria of SbC that was constructed for this study evidence of scripted behavior by the suicidal actor was identified.

Defining SbC
The definition of SbC used for use in this study has allowed for a demarcation between what constitutes an SbC incident, and equally as important, what does not. The presence of all three definitional elements, voluntariness, threat, and communication, must be established in order for an incident to be classified as SbC. Without one or more of these elements a classification of an incident as SbC did not occur. In each of the included cases there was evidence that the suicidal actor voluntarily entered the SbC script. Police tactics were closely scrutinized in order to determine if these tactics were a precipitating factor. Questionable and offensive police tactics resulted in exclusion of 10 (17.5%) of the original

162

cases (N=57) and accounting for over 32% of the excluded cases (n=31). Similarly, the mental state of the actor in these cases was a significant factor in determining voluntariness with an equal representation of excluded cases as in the previous variable. Collectively, these two variables, one demographic the other situational, account for 35% (n=20) of the original cases. Even more significant is the fact that these variables account for over 64% (n=20) of the excluded cases (n=31). The definitional element focusing on the existence of a threat was evident in each of the original cases. This variable is the one common denominator that is present in all of the original cases. As a single variable, evidence of a threat, real or perceived, is grossly insufficient in classifying a case as SbC. Yet, practitioners tend to view this variable myopically, allowing the premise that a person attacking the police is suicidal to cloud an objective analysis of the incident. The third element, communication, was not found in 28% of the original cases (n=16) accounting for the absence of this variable in more than 51% of the excluded cases.

Overall, the definitional construct of SbC developed for this study has been successful in differentiating between cases that have been classified as SbC in a non-scientific, subjective manner, and cases that can withstand scientific measurement.

A conceptual model of SbC

This research proceeded with an expectation of developing a conceptual model of how SbC is viewed by police practitioners in a generalized sense. The exploratory nature of qualitative research offered the opportunity to develop this model through an examination of raw data undiluted by scientific alteration using collective case study analysis. Regardless of the depth and scope of any case analysis conducted in the preliminary case study the cases included in the original N=57 each contained sufficient information to

163

determine if the case met the established SbC definitional criteria for this research. It was this analysis that resulted in the final bifurcation of cases separating between cases that met the established definitional criteria and those that did not. As a result of this bifurcation a single and obvious element in each of the excluded cases was identified. In those cases that were excluded (n=31) the action(s) of the actor in confronting, attacking, or threatening police officers emerged as the prime indicator of suicidal intent. As seen in the previous analysis of the definitional elements of SbC that were constructed for this research, the actions of the actor in the majority of the excluded cases was a significant factor in the original classification of these cases as SbC.

The conceptual model of SbC that emerges from this research is one that is seen more as negative than a positive in the sense that the classifications are based on erroneous beliefs or assumptions of many of the practitioners who participated through the original cases study analysis, and any model that is developed can only be applied to this cohort. Although 26 of the original cases were classified as SbC the fact that this number is 45% of the original N=57 raises the distinct possibility that SbC is not clearly understood by the majority of police practitioners. An accurate portrayal of the perception that does exist is one that focuses narrowly on the actions of the actor often exclusive of an examination or consideration of the actions of the police, the mental state of the actor, and/or the intent of the actor. The development of a conceptual model in this regard than becomes a construct of an antithesis of what SbC has been defined as in this research; an incident involving a suicidal actor who communicates verbally or non-verbally the intent to commit suicide and voluntarily enters the suicidal drama provoking a deadly force response by police.

The limitations in applying this model to generalize the understandings of SbC to police

practitioners as a whole are obvious. The possible and probable explanations range from

the understandable absence of a clear and standardized definition of SbC within the original

cohort to the larger issue in recognizing that police for the most part are action oriented and

limited in their ability, as regulated by law and/or policy, from deviating from the facts of

the case as they exist.

A logical first-step in countering this unbalance is the universal acceptance of a

standardized definition of SbC, a definition that would not be mutually exclusive to law

enforcement and is capable of reaching across the boundaries of law and medicine. If this

consensus is reached, then further research designed to assess a generalized understanding

of the phenomenon can proceed.

Scripted Behavior

The exploratory nature of this research has allowed for an examination of a variable that

has yet to be considered in the SbC drama; scripted behavior. The variable scripted

behavior was constructed for this research with the expectation of identifying the nature of

the cause and effect relationship that exists in a deadly force exchange between the suicidal

actor and the police. Expanding on previous research that identified the existence of

scripted behavior associated with a police response in a deadly force situation this study

applied the principle of script theory to the suicidal actor.

In examining the actions of the suicidal actor in the included cases (n=26) a cause and

effect relationship between the actions of the actor and the actions/reactions of the police

officer(s) in the suicidal drama was identified. In each of these cases the actions of the suicidal actor could be clearly identified as scripted. The actor was identified as a voluntary participant in the suicidal drama and their actions were determined to be provoking for the intended purpose of committing suicide. These incidents and the actions of a suicidal actor are not occurring in a vacuum. It would be logical to assert that if someone is intent on committing suicide, specifically SbC, the completion of that act requires a deadly force response by the police. To achieve this goal the suicidal actor needs to present sufficient and continued provocation until the desired end-state occurs, and this end-state becomes *victim-scripted suicide*. This categorization describes more accurately a suicide that involves the use of a non-cooperating proxy such as a police officer who is placed in the untenable position of being the mechanism of death in this suicidal script.

The limitations in advancing scripted behavior of suicidal actors to the level of a theory based on this research are obvious. With a limited number of cases, this research does not offer the ability to generalize scripted behavior to a larger cohort or population. However, the fact that scripted behavior of the suicidal actor has been identified in 26 cases that were classified as SbC raises the probability that the variable is worthy of further analysis.

DEMOGRAPHIC and SITUATIONAL VARIABLES

The ability to capture information regarding specific demographic and situational variables in the cases under examination in this research was seen as an opportunity to build a foundation for future research on SbC. These variables help to gain a clearer understanding of the dynamics and the nature of SbC incidents, and can help to guide the development of future research in this area. The data is based on a small N=26 and is not intended or expected to be used for generalization.

The demographic variables of the suicidal actors observed in this research were for the most part consistent with frequencies specific to other studies of SbC as well as larger quantitative studies of suicide in general. In this research the vast majority of actors in the SbC drama are male, accounting for 88.5 % of the cases, and the race of a person involved in SbC is more likely to be White (76.9 %) than Black (11.5%) and other nonwhites (11.5%). Equally consistent were frequencies associated with the age of the suicidal actor with the mean for this cohort being 36.92 years of age.

Other demographic variables examined in this research focused on any documented past criminal history of the actor, the marital status of the suicidal actor and the presence of domestic violence, evidence of alcohol and/or drug use, previous suicide attempts, and a documented history of mental illness. Each of these variables was examined in the present research and sufficient frequencies were obtained to allow for a generalized comparison of this study with other studies on SbC and in a limited sense to studies on suicide. However, the gaps in information from file-to-file in this research cannot be ignored.

In examining the frequency of a criminal history of the suicidal actor in this research revealed that in those cases where sufficient information was present to determine criminal history, 50% of the cases involved actors who had a prior criminal history. This finding is also consistent with previous research on SbC. The examination of the marital status of suicidal actors revealed that in 84.6% of the cases where information was available an overwhelming majority of the cases (46.2%) involved actors who were not married by a ratio of more than 2:1 followed by married (19.2%), separated (11.5%), and divorced or widow/widower (3.8%). The remaining 15.4% of the cases (n=4) did not contain sufficient information to determine marital status. The related variable of domestic violence in this study (26.9%) was also consistent with similar research. In reviewing the frequency of alcohol and/or drug use it was found that the majority of cases involved an actor who was more likely to consume and abuse alcohol (61.5%) before and during the incident. Known drug use was evident in a nominal number of the cases (15.4%), a figure that notwithstanding missing data (11.5%) was eclipsed by cases where drug use was not evident (73.1%). Similarly, there was evidence in only three cases (11.5%) of a combination use of alcohol and drugs. The examination of evidence of any previous suicide attempt(s) was one of the variables that were hampered by a significant absence of information from file-to-file. The distribution of known attempts (34.6%), no attempts (34.6%), and missing information (30.8%) was fairly even. Reliance on this information due to a high percentage of cases with missing information would be suspect and unreliable. Future examinations of this variable may prove as equally problematic, but necessary nonetheless. The final demographic variable examined focused on evidence of any psychiatric history of the suicidal actor. A vast majority of cases (65.4%) supported the existence of some type of psychiatric history as well as an equal number of cases that contained a reference to or evidence of a legitimate diagnosis of mental illness. However, as seen with the previous variable the high percentage of cases with missing or incomplete information (30.8%) becomes problematic, and generalization to a larger population is inappropriate.

In reviewing the frequency distributions of the situational variables of crime, police reaction, the presence or absence of family, the location of the incident, weapons, and the continuum of force that were examined in this research similar issues related to the limitations in generalizing this data to a larger cohort are present. In spite of identifiable gaps in information each of these variables is deserving of brief commentary with an eye towards future research.

The examination of the variable crime in this research was difficult for a number of reasons. From an operational perspective this research failed to adequately define the variable. Aside from the fact that SbC in and of itself involves a variety of criminal offenses the variable as used was too broad in scope to accurately capture worthwhile information. However, information was developed in all of the included cases (n=26) that allowed for an identification of cases that involved the commission of a felony or misdemeanor independent of crimes specific to the acts associated with SbC. Ten (38.5%) of the 26 cases involved the commission of a crime prior to the SbC drama. Of these 10, nine of the cases involved the commission of a felony. The situational variable that focused on the involvement of police in the SbC drama examined the reaction(s) of the police as the incident developed in so far as seeking available cover from an assault. This information was often readily identifiable in the various police reports, crime scene sketches, and eyewitness statements. The use of cover by police occurred in a majority of the cases (61.5%) and the most frequent form of cover used was a police vehicle (42.3%). Recorded simultaneously with this variable was a variable designed to measure the frequency of SbC cases involving the element of surprise. Guided by previous SbC research, which found that surprise attacks in SbC incidents occurred in less than 4% of the cases examined, this study anticipated similar results. However, the frequency of surprise attacks in the present research was found to occur in a majority of the cases (57.7%). The variance in these results is understandable considering the differences in data, methodology, and

169

operationalization of the variables, yet this range cannot be overlooked and deserves further analysis. Any future analysis of this variable should consider that this research found that by a ratio of more than 2:1, the element of surprise trumped the ability of police officers to seek available cover.

The presence or absence of family members and the milieu in the SbC incident were recorded simultaneously for the purpose of seeing if there was any relationship between the presence of family members and incidences of SbC occurring in or near the home. This research determined that in the majority of the cases when the incident occurred in or was proximate to the residence family members were present. The implications for future research in this regard should be obvious. Establishing or disproving a nexus between SbC, the presence of family, and the milieu could possibly have legitimate predictive value when taken into consideration with other demographic and situational variables.

This research has found that the use of a weapon, regardless of type, was present in all but two of the total N=26 (92.3%), and in the two cases where a weapon was not visible the suicidal actor intimated or simulated the use of some sort of weapon. The finding that firearms (65.4%) was the predominate weapon of choice, and that handguns (46.2%) followed by shotguns (19.2%) were more often than not the weapon of choice in SbC is consistent with the literature.

The continuum of force employed by the police in the cases examined in the present research is the last variable to be discussed. This variable represents a general range of the varying types of force from the lowest level, Level 1 - constructive force, that involves some form of verbalization to the highest, Level 5 - deadly force, that police are authorized to use based on the nature and extent of a threat. Notwithstanding any level or degree of

surprise all of the included cases (n=26) had evidence of some form of constructive force

used by the police officer(s). The mid-range levels, Level 2 – physical contact, Level 3 –

physical force, and Level 4 – mechanical force, were seldom used by or evident in the

police response. Level 5, or deadly force, occurred in all but one (3.8%) of the cases. This

incident, an attempt, was resolved without the use of deadly force. As with many of the

demographic and situational variables recorded in this research the ability to generalize this

variable to a larger population is limited, yet the results are not without value. Each of these

variables provides sufficient information for a foundation of more probative research that is

necessary to continue the quest for knowledge relative to SbC.

Overall, the final analysis of each of the demographic and situational variable categories in

the present study has shown that these variables are consistent with the literature and it is

likely that future studies of SbC will yield similar results. However, the primary focus of

this research was to examine how police practitioners view the SbC phenomenon in a

generalized sense, and to then develop this generalized view into a conceptual model to be

tested against a definitional construct. What resulted were findings that in 55% of the cases

the submitting officer's classification of the incident failed to meet the SbC definitional

construct. The limitation of this study then rests with the ability of the conceptual model

that was developed to withstand analysis.

The utility of this research has yet to be determined. Recommendations for future research

in this regard are tempered with a caution to seek a standardized definition of SbC, and to

consider that the definition constructed in this study will clearly and narrowly define the phenomenon. If that consideration is plausible, and supported by more substantive

research, then the colloquialism SbC would be more aptly identified as victim-scripted

suicide.

BIBLIOGRAPHY

Abelson, R.P. (1981). Psychological Status of the Script Concept. *American Psychologist*. (36), No. 7, pp. 715-29.

Abbott, R., Young, S., Grant, G., Goward, P., Seager, C., and Ludlow, J. (2003). *Railway Suicide: An Investigation of Individual and Organisational Consequences*. Doncaster: Doncaster and South Humber Healthcare NHS Trust.

Allen, S. W. (1999). Suicide Prevention Training: One Department's Response. In *Suicide and Law Enforcement* (Vol. Section 1, pp. 9-15). Quantico, VA: FBI.

Allen, S. W. (2004). Dynamics in Responding to Departmental Personnel. In V. B. Lord (Ed.), *Suicide by Cop: Inducing Officers to Shoot. Practical Direction for Recognition, Resolution, and Recovery* (pp. 245-257). Flushing, New York: Looseleaf Law Publications, Inc.

Alpert, G. P. (1995). *Police Use of Deadly Force: A Statistical Analysis of the Metro-Dade Police Department*. Washington, DC: Police Executive Research Forum.

Anleu, S. L. (1995). *Deviance, Conformity and Control. 2nd Ed*. Melbourne: Longman.

Anonymous. (1998, September 1). 10% of Police Shootings Found to be Suicide by Cop [Editorial]. *Criminal Justice Newsletter*, pp. 1-2.

Bittner, E. (1970). *The Functions of the Police in Modern Society*. Washington, D.C.: U.S. Government Printing Office.

Bresler, S. (2003). Attempted Suicide by Cop: A Case Study of Traumatic Brain Injury and the Insanity Defense. *Journal of Forensic Science, 48*(1), 190-194.

Brewster, J. (1999). Lessons Learned: A Suicide in a Small Police Department. In *Suicide and Law Enforcement* (Vol. Section 1, pp. 45-56). Quantico, VA: FBI.

Brooks, C. (1991, August 26). Suicide-by-cop is a growing problem in San Diego (As noted in Homant, Kennedy, and Hupp, Journal of Criminal Justice 28 (2000) 43-52. *San Diego Union-Trib*, p. C-1.

Brubaker, L. C. (2002). Deadly Force: A 20-year study of deadly force encounters. *FBI Law Enforcement Bulletin, 71(4), 6-13.*

Callahan,, J. M., Jr. (2003). *Deadly Force: Constitutional Standards, Federal Guidelines and Officer Standards*. Flushing, N.Y.: Looseleaf Law Publications, Inc.

Campbell, B. M. (1986). Excessive Force Claims: Removing the Double Standard. *University of Chicago Law Review, 53*, 1369.

Creswell, J. W. (1998). *Qualitative Inquiry and Research Design: Choosing Among Five Traditions*. Thousand Oaks, CA: Sage Publications, Inc.

Crosby, A. E. (1999). Incidence of Suicidal Ideation and Behavior in the United States, 1994 (Crosby, A.E., Cheltenham, M.P., and Sacks, J.J.). *Suicide and Life-Threatening Behavior, 29*(2), 131-140.

Denzin, N. K. and Lincoln, Y. S. (2003). The Discipline and Practice of Qualitative Research. In N. K. Denzin and Y. S. Lincoln (Eds.), *The Landscape of Qualitative Research: Theories and Issues, 2nd Ed.* (pp. 1-46). Thousand Oaks, CA: Sage Publications, Inc.

DuCharme, S. D. (2002). The Search for Reasonableness in Use-of-Force Cases: Understanding the Effects of Stress on Perception and Performance. *Fordham Law Review, 70,* 2515-2561.

Durkheim, E. (1951). *Suicide: A Study in Sociology.* New York: A Free Press.

Dwyer, W. O., Graesser, A.C., Hopkinson, P.L., and Lupfer, M.B. (1990). Application of Script Theory to Police Officer's Use of Deadly Force. *Journal of Police Science and Administration, 17*(4), 295-301.

Ellis, T. E. (1988). Classification of Suicidal Behavior: A Review and Step Toward Integration. *Suicide and Life-Threatening Behavior, 18*(4), 358-372.

Fridell, S. W. and. L. (1996). Forces of Change on Police Policy: The Impact of Tennessee v. Garner. *American Journal of Police,* 97-110.

Friedrich, R. J. (1980). Police Use of Force: Individuals, Situations, and Organizations. In *The Annals of the Academy of Political and Social Science* (Vol. 452, pp. 83-97). Philadelphia: The American Academy of Political and Social Science.

Futrell, R. H. (1974). *An Empirical Test of a Social Structural Model for the Prediction of Suicide and Homicide.* Ann Arbor, MI: Xerox University Microfilms: Dissertation.

Fyfe, J. J. (personnel communication, December 8, 2004).

Fyfe, J.J. and Blumberg, M. (1985). Response to Griswold: A More Valid Test of the Justifiability of Police Actions. *American Journal of Police* (5), No. 2.

Fyfe, J.J. (1986). The Spilt-Second Syndrome and Other Determinants of Police Violence. In *Violent Transactions.* A.T. Campbell and J.J. Gibbs Eds. Oxford. Basil Blackwell.

Garner, J. (1996). Understanding the Use of Force By and Against the Police by John Buchanan, Tom Schade, and John Hepburn. In *National Institute of Justice: Research Brief* (Vol. NCJ 158614, pp. 1-11). Washington, D.C.: U.S. Department of Justice: Office of Justice Programs/National Institute of Justice.

Geberth, V. J. (1993, July). Suicide-By-Cop. *Law and Order, 41 (7),* 105-109.

Geberth, V. J. (1996). *Practical Homicide Investigation: Tactics, Procedures, and Forensic Techniques.* New York: CRC Press.

Geller, W. A. (1992). *Deadly Force: What We Know. A Practitioner's Desk Reference on Police-Involved Shootings.* Washington, DC: Police Executive Research Forum .

Gentner, D. (1989). Historical shifts in the use of analogy in science. . In B. Gholson (Ed.), *Psychology of Science: Contributions to Metascience.* Cambridge, MA: Cambridge University Press.

Gliatto, M. F. (1999, March 15). Evaluation and Treatment of Patients with Suicidal Ideation/Anil K. Rai. *American Family Physician.* Retrieved February 15, 2004, from http://www.aafp.org/afp/990315ap/1500.html

Goldney, R. Retrieved February 2, 2004, from http://www.suicidology.

Goldsmith, S. K. (Ed.). (2002). *Reducing suicide: A national imperative (TC Pellmar, AM Kleinman, WE Bunney) .* Washington, DC: National Academies Press.

Grella, N. M. (2000). *An Analysis of Suicide-by-Cop Incidents.* New York: John Jay College of

Criminal Justice of the City University of New York.

Hardy, R. E. and Cull, J.G. (1973). *Applied Psychology in Law Enforcement and Corrections.* Springfield, Illinois: Charles C. Thomas.

Harper, R. B. (1983). Accountability of Law Enforcement Officers in the Use of Deadly Force. *Howard Law Journal, 26,* 119.

Hart, C. (2003). *Doing a Literature Review.* London: Sage Publications Ltd.

Hawthorn, G. (1976). *Enlightenment and Despair. A History of Sociology.* London: Cambridge University Press.

Heinsen, D. L. (1999). Suicide and Law Enforcement: Is Suicide Intervention a Necessary Part of Police Training? In *Suicide and Law Enforcement* (Vol. Section 1, pp. 105-113). Quantico, VA: FBI.

Homant, R. J., Kennedy, D.B. (2001). A Typology of Suicide by Police Incidents. In *Suicide and Law Enforcement* (Pp. 577-586). Washington, DC: U.S. Department of Justice, Federal Bureau of Investigation.

Homant, R.J. (2000). "Suicide by Police" in Section 1983 Suits: Relevance of Police Tactics. *University of Detroit Mercy Law Review, 77,* 555.

Homant, R. J., Kennedy, D.B., and Hupp, R.T. (2000). Real and perceived danger in police assisted suicide. *Journal of Criminal Justice, 28,* 43-52.

Honig, A. L. (2001, October). Police Assisted Suicide. *The Police Chief, 68,* 89-92.

Hontz, T. A. (2000). Justifying the Deadly Force Response. *Police Quarterly, 2*(4), 462-476.

Horvath, F. (1987). The Police Use of Deadly Force: A Description of Selected Characteristics of Intrastate Incidents. *Journal of Police Science and Administration, 15*(3), 226-238.

Hutson, H. R., Anglin, D., Yarbrough, J., Hardaway, K., Russell, M., Strote, J. Canter, M., and Blum, B. (1998). Suicide by Cop. *Annals of Emergency Medicine, 32*(6), 665 - 669.

Jacoby, J. E. (Ed.). (1994). *Classics of Criminology 2nd Ed.: Social Structure and Anomie by Robert K. Merton.* Prospect Heights, IL: Waveland Press.

Kachur, S.P., Potter, L.B., James, S.P., and Powell, K. E. (1995). Suicide in the United States: 1980-1992. *Violence Surveillance Summary Series, No.1.* National Center for Injury Prevention and Control. Atlanta, GA.

Karmen, A. (personal communication, December 21, 2004).

Katz, S. R. (1998, April 27). Doctor Assisted Suicide - A Bad Oxymoron and A Bad Idea. *Connecticut Post,* p. Op-Ed.

Kennedy, D. B. (1998). Suicide by Cop. *F.B.I. Law Enforcement Bulletin,* (August), 21-27.

Kennedy, R. J., Homant, R.J., and Hupp, R.T. (2000). Effectiveness of Less Than Lethal Force in Suicide-by-Cop Incidents. *Police Quarterly, 3*(2), 153-171.

Keram, E. A. (2001). Suicide by Cop: Issues in Outcome and Analysis. In D. C. Sheehan (Ed.), *Suicide and Law Enforcement* (pp. 587-617). Washington, DC: U.S. Department of Justice, Federal Bureau of Investigation.

Kinnaird, B. A. (2003). *Use of Deadly Force: Expert Guidance for Decisive Force Response*. Flushing, NY: LooseLeaf Law Publications.

Klinger, D. A. (2001). Suicidal Intent in Victim-Precipitated Homicide: Insights from the Study of "Suicide by Cop". *Homicide Studies, 5*(3), 206-226.

Kreitman, N. (1988). The Two Traditions in Suicide Research (The Dublin Lecture). *Suicide and Life-Threatening Behavior, 18*(1), 66-72.

Lardner, J. (2000). *NYPD A City and Its Police*. New York: Henry Holt and Company.

Lindsay, M. S. (2001). Identifying the Dynamics of Suicide by Cop. In D. C. Sheehan (Ed.), *Suicide and Law Enforcement* (pp. 619-616). Washington, DC: U.S. Department of Justice, Federal Bureau of Investigation.

Lord, V. B. (2004). Suicide by Cop Incidents in North Carolina: A Comparison of Successful and Unsuccessful Cases. In V. B. Lord (Ed.), *Suicide by Cop: Inducing Officers to Shoot. Practical Direction for Recognition, Resolution, and Recovery* (pp. 13-29). Flushing, New York: Looseleaf Law Publications, Inc.

Lord, V. B. (1999). Law Enforcement-Assisted Suicide: Characteristics of Subjects and Law Enforcement Intervention Techniques. In S. and. Waoten (Ed.), *Suicide and Law Enforcement* (pp. 617-625). Washington, D.C.: U.S. Department of Justice, Federal Bureau of Investigation.

Lord, V. B. (2000). Law Enforcement-Assisted Suicide. *Criminal Justice Behavior, 27*(3), 401-419.

Luna, J. K. (2002). *Circumstances and Behaviors of Suicide by Cop*. Ann Arbor, Michigan: UMI Dissertation Services.

Lunden, W.A. (1973). *Emile Durkheim (1858-1917)*. In *Pioneers in Criminology*. Herman Mannheim (Ed.). Montclair, NJ: Patterson Smith.

Marshall, C. (1989). *Designing Qualitative Research Gretchen B. Rossman*. Newbury Park, CA: Sage Publications Inc.

McGuinness, M. (2002). Law Enforcement Use of Force: The Objective Reasonableness Standards Under North Carolina and Federal Law. *The Campbell Law Review, 24*, 201.

Mohandie, K. and Meloy, J.R. (2000). Clinical and Forensic Indicators of "Suicide by Cop". *Journal of Forensic Science, 45*(2), 384-389.

Merton, R. K. (1968). *Social Theory and Social Structure*. New York: The Free Press.

Meyer, R. G. (1992). *Abnormal Behavior and the Criminal Justice System*. San Francisco: Lexington Books.

Miller, R. D. (2001). Suicide by cop and criminal responsibility. *The Journal of Psychiatry and Law, 29*(3), 295-328.

Morton, L. L. (2001). Suicide and gay/lesbian/bisexual youth: implications for clinicians (Jeff L'Heureux). *Journal of Adolescence, 24*, 39-49.

Parent, R. B. (2004). Police Use of Deadly Force in the Pacific Northwest: Victim-Precipitated

Homicide. In V. B. Lord (Ed.), *Suicide by Cop: Inducing Officers to Shoot. Practical Direction for Recognition, Resolution, and Recovery* (pp. 31-54). Flushing, New York: Looseleaf Law Publications, Inc.

Parent, R. B. (2001). Suicide by Cop in North America: Victim-Precipitated Homicide. In D. C. Sheehan (Ed.), *Suicide and Law Enforcement* (pp. 653-662). Washington, DC: U.S. Department of Justice, Federal Bureau of Investigation.

Parent, R. B. (1998, October). Suicide by Cop: Victim-precipitated homicide. *The Police Chief, 65,* 111-114.

Parent, R. B. (1996). *Aspects of Police Use of Deadly Force in British Columbia: The Phenomenon of Victim-Precipitated Homicide.* Ann Arbor, Michigan: UMI Dissertation.

Paynter, R. L. (2000, June). Suicide by Cop. *Law Enforcement Technology, 27,* 40-44.

Pinnizotta, A. J., Davis, E. F., and Miller, C. E. (2005). Suicide by cop: A Devastating Dilemma. *FBI Law Enforcement Journal, 74*(2), 8-20.

Office of Juvenile Justice and Delinquency Prevention. (2004). *Juvenile Suicides, 1981-1998* (NCJ 196978).

Pyers, L. C. (2001, July/August, 2001). Suicide by Cop-The Ultimate "Trap". *The FBI National Academy Associates Magazine, 3, No.4.*

Rickgarn, R. L. V. (2001). Victim-Precipitated Homicide: Incident and Aftermath. In D. C. Sheehan (Ed.), *Suicide and Law Enforcement* (pp. 677- 687). Washington, DC: U.S. Department of Justice, Federal Bureau of Investigation.

Roberts, J. E. (2001). Suicide by Cop Syndrome: How Law Enforcement Successfully Can Meet the Challenge. In D. C. Sheehan (Ed.), *Suicide and Law Enforcement* (pp. 689-693). Washington, DC: U.S. Department of Justice, Federal Bureau of Investigation.

Rumbaut, R. G. (1979). Changing Conceptions of the Police Role: A Sociological Review. *Crime and Justice: An Annual Review of Research by Egon Bittner* (Vol. 1, pp. 239-288). Chicago: University of Chicago.

Shanoo, T. K. (1990). *Helping Your Child Cope with Depression and Suicidal Thoughts.* New York: Lexington Books.

Sherman, L. W. (1980). Perspectives on Police and Violence. In R. D. Lambert (Ed.), *The Annals of the American Academy of Political and Social Science: The Police and Violence* (pp. 1-12). Philadelphia: The American Academy of Political and Social Science.

Shneidman, E. (1996). *The suicidal mind. In Mehandie and Meloy.* New York: Oxford University Press.

Simon, T.R., Swann, A.C., Powell, K. E., Potter, L.B., Kresnow, M., and O'Carroll, P.W. Characteristics of Impulsive Suicide Attempts and Attempters. *Suicide and Life-Threatening Behavior* (Volume 32. pp. 49-59). The American Association of Suicidology.

Simpson, G. (Ed.). (1951). *Suicide: A Study in Sociology.* New York: A Free Press.

Singleton, R. A. (1999). *Approaches to Social Research/ Bruce Straits.* New York: Oxford Press.

Stake, R. E. (2003). Case Studies. In N. K. Denzin and Y. S. Lincoln (Eds.), *Strategies of Qualitative*

Inquiry (pp. 134 - 164). Thousand Oaks, CA: Sage.

Stewart, A. (2004, May 27). Study: Suicide is Jersey's 3rd-leading cause of death. *Star Ledger*, p. 48, Warren, Sussex, and Morris.

Unknown. (2004). Suicide: A Suicidological Definition. In *ASBS*. Retrieved February 15, 2004, from http://ashbusstop.org/sui_def_suicidology.html.

Unnithan, N. P. (1994). *The Currents of Lethal Violence: An Integrated Model of Suicide and Homicide*. Albany, New York: State University of New York Press.

U.S. Department of Justice. (1999). *Use of Force by Police: Overview of National and Local Data* (NCJ-176330). Washington, DC: National Institute of Justice.

U.S. Department of Justice. (1996). *National Data Collection on Police Use of Force* (NCJ-161113). Alexandria, VA: National Institute of Justice.

Vollmer, A. (1972). *The Police and Modern Society*. Montclair, NJ: Patterson Smith.

Wallace, R. A. (2000). Anomie Theory. In *Encyclopedia of Criminology and Deviant Behavior* (Vol. 1, pp. 20-26). Ann Arbor, MI: Brunner-Rutledge.

Williams, G. H. (1993). Controlling the Use of Non-Deadly Force: Policy and Practice. *Harvard BlackLetter Journal, 10,* 79.

Wilson, E. F. (1998). Homicide or Suicide: The Killing of Suicidal Persons by Law Enforcement Officers . *Journal of Forensic Sciences, 43*(1), 46-52.

Wolfgang, M. E. (1961). Suicide by Means of Victim-Precipitated Homicide. *Journal of Clinical and Experimental Psychopathology and Quarterly Review of Psychiatry and Neurology, 20*(4), 335-349.

Wolfgang, M. E. (1975). *Patterns in Criminal Homicide*. Montclair, N.J.: Patterson Smith.

Yarmey, A. D. (1990). *Understanding Police and Police Work*. New York: New York University Press.

von Hentig, H. (1979). *The Criminal and His Victim: Studies in the Sociology of Crime*. New York: Schocken Books.

von Hentig, H. (1948). The Criminal and His Victim. In J. E. Jacoby (Ed.), *Classics of Criminology* (pp. 32-33). Prospect Heights, IL: Waveland Press, Inc.

CPSIA information can be obtained
at www.ICGtesting.com
Printed in the USA
LVOW04s2310181017
552969LV00013B/283/P

9 783836 428422